Wendy Jago has a varied and extensive experience of helping people manage their mammoths. This includes teaching at Sussex and Brighton Universities (academic mammoths), in-service education and mid-life retraining (identity, interpersonal and life-balance mammoths), psychotherapy (including childhood, relationship-based, habit-related, traumatic and performance mammoths), executive coaching in international companies, both private and public sector (managerial mammoths), riding and dressage judging (communication and competition mammoths). And of course she has plenty of personal and domestic mammoths of her own.

She has co-written five seminal books about Neuro-Linguistic Programming (NLP), including the best-selling *The NLP Coach*. Her most recent book, *The NLP Brain Builder*, has already been translated into several languages. As a rider and dressage judge, she pioneered the application of NLP to the complex field of communication in rider–horse partnerships. She now divides her time between coaching and writing.

For more information about Wendy and her work, go to www.pivotalcoaching.co.uk, or for specific enquiries about personal or organisational coaching, contact her directly through wendy@pivotalcoaching.co.uk.

Also by Wendy Jago

The NLP Coach
(with Ian McDermott)

Your Inner Coach
(with Ian McDermott)

The Coaching Bible
(with Ian McDermott)

The NLP Brain Builder

How to
MANAGE
Your
MAMMOTH

The procrastinator's guide
to getting things done

Wendy Jago

piatkus

PIATKUS

First published in Great Britain in 2012 by Piatkus

A CIP catalogue record for this book
is available from the British Library.

The case studies in this book have been written with the knowledge
and permission of my clients and/or with names, places and other
key details changed where necessary to preserve confidentiality.

ISBN 978-0-7499-5735-3

Typeset in Palatino by M Rules
Printed and bound in Great Britain by
Clays Ltd, St Ives plc

Illustrations by Kathryn Rosa Miller

Papers used by Piatkus are from well-managed forests
and other responsible sources.

MIX
Paper from
responsible sources
FSC
www.fsc.org   FSC® C104740

Piatkus
An imprint of
Little, Brown Book Group
100 Victoria Embankment
London EC4Y 0DY

An Hachette UK Company
www.hachette.co.uk

www.piatkus.co.uk

For my husband Leo, who for more than forty years has partnered and supported me in the challenges and the satisfactions of all my mammoth-managing. My love always.

Contents

Contents

Introduction

You thought that mammoths were extinct? Forget it! We all have at least one or two in our lives; and they can be overwhelming, if we don't have ways of managing them. But take comfort – because this book is your own personal pocket guide to mammoth-managing.

Mammoths are everywhere!

There are many different kinds of mammoth and they manifest in all areas of our lives. Here are some common ones.

- A task or chore that needs doing
- A dream that hasn't been realised
- Sorting through possessions
- An obligation or debt that needs discharging
- A wrong that rankles
- An ambition that hasn't been achieved
- A job you 'haven't time for'

- A habit that's difficult to break
- Creating a plan or strategy for the future.

You will almost certainly recognise many of these mammoths. Are you giving them any house-room, head-room or heart-room?

Your mammoth

Mammoths can be practical or intellectual, tangible or intangible, and virtually all of them will seem even larger than they actually are because they involve your feelings and beliefs. The more vital these are to you, the bigger your mammoth will seem.

As the strategies of mammoth-managing are essentially the same whatever kind of mammoth you're dealing with, I'm going to refer throughout the book to 'your mammoth', rather than specifying the type of mammoth it may be. You will know if what you are dealing with is a task, a plan, a chore or an obligation, and that's what matters.

Mammoths make us feel out of control

Just like their hairy predecessors, mammoths can make us feel puny and inadequate. But, as I've discovered over many years of helping people with their mammoth issues at work and at home, the way you perceive your mammoth is the key. Something that's a mammoth to you may seem quite small and harmless to someone else – and vice versa.

The seventeenth-century Royalist poet Richard Lovelace wrote:

> Stone walls do not a prison make
> Nor iron bars a cage.

Though his body was imprisoned, Lovelace knew that his *mind* was what determined how he felt. And the same goes for mammoths.

Many years ago, I saw a cartoon showing a cavewoman standing by the body of a mammoth. She was saying to herself, 'And the week after that, mammoth stew ... and the month after that, mammoth soup ...' She wasn't fazed by her mammoth, because she knew she could cut it down to size, bit by bit. (She could also make something nourishing and tasty out of it, and that's another interesting implication: once tamed, mammoths can have surprisingly beneficial outcomes.)

Mammoths don't have to be scary monsters, if you know the right way to deal with them. And there's a lot in this book about just that – how your mammoth is framed in your mind and how it can be reframed to make it more approachable.

The message of this book is straightforward and reassuring: *mammoths can be managed*. And once you've got your thinking sorted, the practical way to get your mammoth under control is the same one the cavewoman used: breaking it into chunks. Or, as I prefer to think of them, bite-sized pieces.

Bite-sizing and NLP

Chunking is a concept that comes from a very practical body of knowledge known as Neuro-Linguistic Programming (NLP), and it describes the process of breaking large things down into smaller components, or building up small components in order to create something large. When I'm coaching and teaching, I tend to use the NLP phrases 'chunking up' and 'chunking down' to refer to things like eating away at a big problem small mouthful by small mouthful or building incrementally up to a big achievement. I use the phrase 'bite-sizing' when I'm referring to working out what is the *right-sized* chunk for you, as an individual, to work with. You may naturally be more comfortable with small chunks, or alternatively, with larger ones. Bite-sizing is the art of getting the right-sized chunks and that's the key to success when you're dealing with mammoths.

How NLP came about

NLP was developed in America in the 1970s as a result of studying in great detail how very effective therapists went about their work. (For more information, see 'Explore NLP' in the Further Explorations section, p. 221.) Though they began by studying people working in a particular field, the NLP researchers and developers soon realised that their discoveries about excellence applied to any and every profession or activity. They found that excellence depended not just on what outstanding practitioners *did*, but also on how they *thought* and *communicated* with others and within themselves. From their study, the developers isolated many underlying processes, strategies and sequences which have successfully been applied to help people cultivate excellence in many fields such as education, the performance arts and business and, indeed, all forms of communication. NLP's findings are about *how* thinking and behaviour actually happen, rather than *what* issue or topic they are concerned with, so it can be applied in all walks of life. NLP isn't theoretical: you don't have to start at the beginning or attempt to learn it all. You can use just a bit of it – such as bite-sizing or chunking.

NLP concepts and strategies are drawn from what works at deep, not surface levels. The surface detail of work and home will be different, of course, but the principles and the underlying structures are the same – just as the structure of the human body is the same across race, age and culture. That's how fundamental NLP is. It gives us a working map of brainwork.

How chunking can help you

Chunking can become an indispensable tool for improving your life.

You may have picked up this book in the hope that it will help you with a mammoth at work. Chunking can help you with planning, presenting, projects, people and performance. Or you may have reached for it as a potential ally in mammoth struggles in your personal life. Chunking can help there too. And my bite-sizing strategies can help you refine your chunking even further.

As you read on, you'll find examples from both the work and private lives of my clients. Do examples have to match your situation in order to help you? No, they don't. You can get really useful information for a work mammoth from reading about someone else's home mammoth (and vice versa) because the processes that underlie each are the same: how you think, what you do, how you feel – and how each of these interconnects with and affects the others. And for exactly the same reason, the chunking and bite-sizing strategies I explore in this book apply to each and every kind of mammoth you might face, whatever its nature and context.

How will this book help you?

This book is itself an example of chunking down. It breaks the seemingly massive task of managing mammoths down into do-able processes.

- Section One helps you identify the kind of mammoth you are personally dealing with, pinpoint *exactly* what's been preventing you from managing it up till now and understand your own characteristic ways of going about things and use them to your best advantage. It also takes you through a checklist of what every mammoth-manager needs to know.

- Section Two looks at some common mammoths that are best tamed by a chunking-down approach: doing those chores, finding your way through big tasks and complex problems, freeing yourself from the weight of obligations and laying to rest mammoths left over from the past.

- Section Three takes a chunking-up approach to building new or better habits, realising dreams and achievements and creating the you that you'd prefer to be.

- Section Four adds the icing to the cake. Every strategy can be used more or less effectively – so how much more can you achieve when you make full use of both your peak-energy times and your natural times for rest, healing and reflection?

    The book ends with a reminder that achieving all of this needn't take mammoth amounts of time or energy: even scraps of available time used well are enough to provide the leverage needed to achieve what I call 'twenty-minute miracles'.

My background and experience

One of the great delights of a long and varied career is that I've been able to work with and learn from a huge variety of different people on wide-ranging issues.

My early career as an administrator gave me real insight into the challenges faced by middle managers in large organisations. More recently, coaching senior managers in business and in the public sector showed me how important it is to understand the way organisations work, how teams and hierarchies operate and what qualities are needed to communicate with others effectively and influence them with integrity.

In my years as a trainer of teachers and psychotherapists, I learned the importance of identifying the 'building blocks' of understanding and the 'stepping stones' that enable people to make reliable progress in learning and achieving. Running my own psychotherapy practice for nearly twenty years after that enabled me to appreciate the vulnerabilities hidden in even the most successful and senior people, as well as the anguish and conflict that ordinary, everyday life with families and friends can bring. In particular, the understanding of unconscious processes of learning, mind–body interaction and natural healing gained through working with hypnotic and other specialised 'altered' states of consciousness has allowed me to appreciate and marvel at the extent to which important personal changes can happen when people learn to listen to themselves and work according to their own rhythms and qualities.

This book draws on this invaluable range of experiences to offer you practical, yet transformational, strategies for getting things done, making things happen and moving things forward. Perhaps most significantly, it distils the secrets of self-management which underlie the eventual taming of all mammoths, however daunting they may at first appear to be. And, in the course of it, I'm going to challenge some common and debilitating assumptions by showing you that managing mammoth issues, facing

mammoth challenges and creating mammoth achievements need not be a mammoth task, involve great difficulty
or take up huge amounts of effort and time.

How to use this book

This is a guide book: it provides important information to
help you find your way around the territory that is you. You
needn't read it through from beginning to end, but you'll certainly find it helpful to read Section One (which sets the scene
for taming all types of mammoth) and Section Four (which
will help you discover how you can become even more
subtle and effective by working with your natural energy
flow and using small windows of opportunity to bring about
miracles of change). Sections Two and Three are focused on
applying the key mammoth-taming strategies to commonly
occurring mammoths and allow you to get straight to work
on the specific mammoth that's troubling you.

To get the best from the book, you'll need not only to read
the relevant exercises, but also to do them. You'll have to
take a good, honest look at yourself, and you may have to
accept that from time to time you have contributed to keeping your mammoth alive, even if you didn't create it in the
first place. That's only human.

There is no catch-all 'recipe' for tidiness, efficiency,
people-management or effective communication, but what
this book will do is help you to expose the processes
through which, if you choose to apply them, you can
achieve any or all of these.

Happy mammoth-taming!

How to
MANAGE
Your
MAMMOTH

SECTION ONE

Know Your Mammoth

1

First Spot Your Mammoth

Something that's a huge task or burden to you may be a straightforward chore to someone else or a breeze to someone else again. Sometimes, it can help to know that not everyone experiences it as you do – but not if that makes you feel even more inadequate. It's important that you respect your own perceptions: *for you*, it's a genuine mammoth. It's *your* feelings about it and *your* sense of the difficulty it poses for you that give you the scale you need to work with. And it is you who have to confront it.

Mammoths disempower us. It's not just their size. There are practical questions to consider, like: how and where do you start to approach and manage them? Which bit of your mammoth issue do you first grab at to make a start? Which bit threatens you most? How difficult will it be to bring the beast to heel? How much time and energy might it take? And there is another, often more hidden, question: what feelings does your mammoth arouse in you? What fears, hopes and past experiences does it carry in its huge bulk?

Common assumptions about managing mammoths

Once you've acknowledged that your issue, challenge or goal is indeed a mammoth as far as you are concerned, and you've stopped feeling guilty about that, you're in a position to whittle away some widely shared assumptions you may have about what managing mammoths involves. Assumptions aren't facts, but there are some commonly held ones that often make mammoths seem bigger than they are. Challenging these can help you see your mammoth (task, challenge, ambition) more clearly and accurately. In itself, this is likely to start the process of cutting it down to size.

> **The way we think about mammoths can make them seem larger (or smaller) than they really are.**

Myths about mammoths

Myth: Managing a mammoth will be difficult and take a huge amount of energy.

Fact: Mammoths can usually be managed with relatively small amounts of energy, if it's judiciously applied. As Archimedes said, 'Give me a lever and a place to stand and I can move the world.'

Myth: The bigger the mammoth, the more difficult it will be to get it to come to heel, and the more time it will probably take.

Fact: Feelings make up a large part of your mammoth: it gets a lot smaller once you've dealt with them.

Myth: Mammoths are enemies.

Fact: A mammoth is in itself neither hostile nor friendly.

Once these extra layers of unhelpful assumptions have been stripped away, mammoths usually begin to shrink and seem less menacing. Now it's time to have a closer look at yours.

So just what kind of mammoth are you dealing with?

Even if two mammoths look alike, they may be subtly – or even greatly – different. I'm going to follow the examples of two of my clients through this chapter as I tease out some important mammoth identification features you can be looking out for yourself.

Ed and Lucy were health professionals, and on the face of it they had the same mammoth: writing up the case studies that were an essential part of their work.

Ed had just one case study to write up as part of his qualifying exam. He spent hours thinking about the client, the possible choices of treatment he had considered, the philosophies that underpinned each of these and the way the client had responded when he actually got started. Somehow, he had to get all of this written up clearly, logically and professionally within a word limit that had, at first, seemed dauntingly large, but that began to feel impossibly short once he actually got going. His kitchen table was covered with books and papers, he had numerous false starts on his computer and the deadline was getting nearer and nearer. *I'm never going to make it*, he thought. *And if I can't make this bit, I won't qualify, however good I may be at actually treating my patients.*

Lucy had been in practice for a number of years and had a busy case load, but no consistent secretarial or administrative support. Though she was good at the face-to-face client work, a lot of her time was taken up with arranging (and changing) appointments. Writing up her case notes was the bit that always seemed to get squeezed out, however good her intentions. She would often end up working into the evenings or weekends, and even though this extra time helped her to catch up a bit, the longer the interval between treating the client and writing the notes, the scrappier the result seemed to be. Her jottings were illegible or didn't make sense when she tried to reread them later. Lucy began to lose faith in more than just her note-taking: *how can I expect to be treated like a professional, if I can't do this fundamental bit?* she thought. *I'm just a fraud.*

Were Ed and Lucy dealing with the same type of mammoth? Actually, they weren't.

Ed's mammoth was a *practical* one: organising and presenting his material. What was there, and how could it be disciplined, ordered and presented? Lucy's mammoth *seemed* to be practical – the lack of administrative support, the need to juggle time and focus, the way colleagues so easily derailed her with requests that seemed legitimate, all squeezing out the time for note-taking and writing up. But actually, her mammoth was one of *emotion* because her difficulties made her feel she was inadequate.

Different issues require different strategies. Ed needed to chunk his mammoth (the finished case study) down into specific headings, so he could put them in order and work on them one by one. In order to bypass the logical, sequential way of thinking that was getting him stuck, I got him to brainstorm headings very quickly. It took him about twenty minutes to jot down what he should cover (including some ideas he hadn't previously thought of), then about the same length of time to work out the order in which the points should be presented. After that, it took only a few hours to actually write it.

Lucy needed strategies for rebuilding her self-confidence as a professional and for staying focused and managing her time more effectively. She also had to accept that asking for help wasn't necessarily a sign of weakness. We worked on this over a period of time, as a result of which she started to feel more confident, arranged for some regular support for her admin and client work and built a new habit of keeping current notes up to date, while picking away at finalising old ones. Because her mammoth was complex and laden with emotion, she required a range of techniques to get it in order and keep it there. It was likely that Lucy would always prefer the face-to-face part of her work, but she learned that by vigilant self-monitoring and regular small attentions it could be kept in order. The practical strategy she needed was to look out for small here-and-now things she could do that would keep her mammoth under control. In addition, a new 'thinking' strategy which placed note-taking as an essential element of her professionalism changed her feelings about doing it and enabled her to get it done.

Build a profile of your mammoth

As these examples show, the 'story' of your mammoth – the detail of what it consists of and how it challenges you – is not enough in itself to help you identify it accurately or effectively manage it. You need to look for the processes it involves and the way it impacts on the structure of your life. It's a bit like identifying birds: a relatively small number are instantly recognisable by their shape or colour, but many look pretty much alike. Learning to observe the details of structure and behaviour helps you compare individuals and identify them accurately. That's how it is with mammoths too.

The more you know about your own mammoth, the more effective you can be in finding the right strategies to deal with it.

Here are some questions that will help you. Some people like to write their answers down, both as a record for now and as a benchmark for evaluating how they progress with taming their beast.

1. Does your mammoth already exist and need completing or is it something that needs to be started and then achieved?

The best way to finish something off once you've started it is by breaking (chunking) it down and finishing it bit by bit (Section Two shows you how to apply this technique to different kinds of commonly occurring mammoth). And the best way to *achieve* or attain something is by building up to it (chunking up), which is applied to different kinds of ambition in Section Three.

2. Does your mammoth relate to the past, the present or the future?

You can't change what happened in the past (I call these 'historical' mammoths and there's more about them in Chapter 8), but you can change how you think and feel about it. Current habits of action or emotion that originated in the past can either be dismantled piece by piece or deliberately supplanted by the creation of new and better habits. And things that haven't happened yet – either ones you dread or ones you want to make happen – may be approached by chunking either up or down.

3. Is your mammoth simple or complex?

Even an apparently simple-task mammoth may have some hidden characteristics. For example, it turned out that Ed's practical difficulties in planning and writing his case study (see pp. 7–8) were made greater by his perfectionist belief that he should include everything that might be relevant. We needed to hammer out what would be a 'good-enough' standard to aim for, and he needed to understand and accept that aiming for perfection can sometimes involve doing more than is actually required.

4. Is your mammoth practical or emotional?
Mammoths often carry hidden emotional freight. Unrecognised or buried feelings, fears and past experiences can be a large part of what's causing your reluctance to get started on even simple, practical tasks. Something that on the surface seems eminently straightforward can get held up by what you un-consciously expect to happen as a result of doing it. These kinds of mammoths are explored in Chapter 2.

5. Is your mammoth specific to one area of your life or several?
Even if it seems pretty clear that your mammoth only occurs in one area, check this out by asking yourself whether it might also be occurring less obviously elsewhere. For example, your mammoth might be that you're afraid of fail-ing or 'being found out' as inadequate at work; but the chances are that this may also, to some degree, be affecting how you feel about yourself vis-à-vis the demands and expectations of family life and friendships.

Practical mammoths can sometimes feature only in one area: for example, you might find it easy to focus on work-related tasks when you are working from home, but get distracted when you are actually at work. Or perhaps you find it easy to work in the company of colleagues, but get distracted when you are at home. By comparing and contrasting like this, you can often discover what NLP calls 'the difference that makes the difference' – which may be your starting place for managing your mammoth more effectively.

Going back to Ed (see pp. 7–8), his perfectionist standards applied in every aspect of his life, and learning to ask himself what would be a 'good-enough' standard with regard to work turned out to be a useful filter for assessing other areas of his life and questioning what 'good enough' might mean – for example, in terms of his relationships, leisure activities and life goals.

6. How does your mammoth hamper your ability to get on with your life and enjoy it?
Answering this question will tell you just how much energy, time and sense of self your mammoth may be swallowing up, and give you a real, immediate incentive to get some of that energy back, so you can put it to work in ways that are more productive and feel more enjoyable.

By now, you should have a pretty full description of your particular mammoth and the effects it is having on your life. Now you need to work out just what's stopping you dealing with it – and that's what we'll be looking at in the next chapter.

2

What Stops You Managing It?

If you have 'been meaning' to do something about a mammoth for ages without actually making a start, then almost certainly *something is actively stopping you*.

> **Your mammoth is not just the undone task, but also whatever stops you getting on with it.**

Your mammoth may involve practical things, relationships with other people or the way you think and feel about yourself. Whichever of these you are facing, feelings such as anxiety, shame or embarrassment are usually a good indicator that more is involved than just your time, energy or indolence.

Don't condemn yourself for feeling like this, but instead take a good, respectful, careful look at these feelings and be inquisitive about what may be causing them.

So what stops you dealing with your mammoth?

It can be a belief, a fear, a feeling or even what you think might happen if you did succeed in dealing with it. Even achievements have their consequences, and disturbing the status quo can feel highly risky and frightening at times. Once you have pinpointed your blockage (and it's rarely a real surprise when you do), the way forward usually becomes more straightforward, and even large or complex mammoths can be broken down into manageable bits (joints and cutlets).

> **When you attack the mammoth's meaning, taming it becomes so much easier.**

First of all, stop lecturing yourself about what you ought to be doing and blaming yourself for not doing it. Everyone feels defensive when they're being put in the wrong – even if they themselves are the ones doing it! There are always good reasons for bad behaviour: now it's time to find out what yours are. Start being the investigator instead of the judge.

What kinds of reasons may be involved?

There are a number of common possibilities. Finding out which is holding you back is the first step to moving forward again.

Know Your Mammoth

1. You may be putting off tackling your mammoth because you believe you have to be in the 'right frame of mind'.

It's easy to assume that special conditions or a special frame of mind are needed to start doing something about your mammoth. Maybe you feel you need privacy, or a certain amount of time to make any progress with it. Perhaps you think you need to be calm, or less stressed, or more courageous before you begin. Actually, you don't.

You don't have to wait for the 'right moment' or 'a good opportunity'. A state of mind is just how you are at any given time and, as such, involves physiological and even biological processes. So changing *anything* about the way you think, feel or behave changes the whole package that makes up your state. And a mental or emotional change can most easily be started by making a physical one.

TRY ONE OF THESE:

- If you are sitting, get up and run on the spot for a minute.
- If you are standing, take a deep breath and, as you do so, clench all your muscles. Then slump and let everything go.
- If you can't do anything this obvious because other people may be watching, stare into space and allow your eyes to defocus.

Then, do just one thing about your mammoth. Here are some examples:

▶

- Make a phone call.
- Send an email.
- Write a list or draw a mind or thought map (there's more about these on pp. 148–9).
- If you need someone else to help you tackle it, your first 'one thing' might simply be to ask yourself which of your friends, colleagues and family members you could ask.

2. You've got so used to your mammoth that you don't even realise you've got choices about it.

Even 'bad' situations and bad habits can get 'comfortable', just because you're familiar with them. You might be used to a bad relationship at work or at home, or to feeling anxious, or you might have got into the habit of running yourself ragged by taking on more than you can chew as a way of coping with life.

Being used to a feeling or a pattern of behaviour can mean that you don't spot real small, do-able opportunities to change things. I call these 'choice-points' – moments when you could take off in a different and better direction. Pretend you are a stranger from another planet investigating the curious behaviour of the alien being that is you! Taking a 'stranger's view' of familiar patterns and feelings and putting them under your mental microscope is a really good way to begin disentangling which ones are part of your mammoth or helping to support its existence. A good, curious, analytical self-examination can usually help you notice choice-points you've been missing up till now.

Know Your Mammoth

In the workplace, for instance, people often put up with something or someone that upsets or irritates them because they may think that everyone has their little foibles, so they should 'just grin and bear it', or that most jobs have their downsides, but 'at least it pays the mortgage'. But as true as these statements may be, thinking this way can be part of what keeps a mammoth like feeling anxious, undervalued, bored or frustrated in place. By highlighting the choices you have actually made day by day, you may start to discover some manoeuvring room you didn't realise you had. Here's an example:

My client, Chris, said he had no 'real reason to be fed up', except that he'd worked at the same job in a large company for a number of years and no longer felt challenged by it. Promotion wasn't a possibility. He and his manager grated on one another, so being at work was often quite stressful, yet the conditions of service were good enough to stop him thinking of leaving. Like many able people, Chris felt that the longer he put up with this situation the less committed and effective he was likely to become. He had got used to the situation, and putting up with it had become a habit in itself.

Once I raised the question of choice-points and we started trying to identify ones he might have missed, Chris realised he'd overlooked a choice-point that could give him a way out: he'd never thought of transferring to another job within the firm. So he'd never glanced at the jobs listed on the company's internal website, never talked with HR about the possibility and never asked around among colleagues in different teams and departments.

Here's a different, and very common example of how unwanted patterns can become habits when choice-points are being ignored. Many people struggle – often for years – with weight loss. It's safe to say that no one deliberately sets out to become overweight. The kilos creep up gradually, through millions of mini-choices every single day: choices about what to eat, what to drink, how often, how much, and about exercise. And somewhere along the line, feelings about being fat, or about the difficulty of doing anything about it, or about how long it would take to make a difference, or about the probability of feeling deprived, all add to the twin mammoths of being overweight and trying to do something about it.

I've worked with many people who wanted to lose weight. The very complexity of reasons and lifestyle patterns that lead to weight problems also mean that there are lots of potential opportunities for making different choices and heading off in other directions. As Lao-Tze, the founder of Daoism, is reputed to have said: the longest journey begins with a single step.

The aim of identifying your choice-points is to help you discover possible junctions to 'branch lines' that could lead you in other directions. Many people who struggle with their weight try to make themselves eat *less* frequently, for example by skipping breakfast or lunch. In fact, it's been shown that eating *more often* would help them feel less hungry and less inclined to eat too much when they did. It's been established that five mini-meals a day is a much better bet than three big ones because they keep blood sugar more constant and thus make it much less likely that you will eat more than you actually need. Another choice-point comes at midday and in the evening, allowing you to adjust the relative balance between the amounts of food you eat at those times.

Small lunch + large evening meal = calories are less likely to be burned off, so more likely to be converted into flab

Big lunch + smaller evening meal = your body has more chance to burn off the food eaten during the day

Here are some other practical choice-points for someone with a weight-related mammoth:

- Whether to skip breakfast or not.
- Having or not having a mid-morning croissant or chocolate bar, downing a few pints or glasses of wine over a business lunch, taking a second or third helping at mealtimes.
- Tidying up your kids' leftovers because it's wicked to waste.
- Using smaller plates as a way of controlling portion size.

Thinking patterns are often so habitual that we don't realise their power to lock us in. Have a good listen to what you're inwardly saying to yourself about your problem. Spotting and changing the thinking that underpins the actual decisions you make can be the first step towards changing them. Every time you catch yourself thinking in a way that maintains your current, problematic eating patterns helps you uncover potential choice-points for thinking differently, so erodes one of the props that keep unwanted patterns in place.

TRY THIS:

Whatever your mammoth may be, look out for choice-points as you go through today. What decisions are you making – and how are you justifying them to yourself? Jot them down. Reflect on them overnight. Once you have brought a choice-point into awareness, you will find it hard, if not impossible, to continue doing what you have always done before – unless, of course, you *choose* to do it!

Let's look again at how thinking can support a continuing weight issue. Are you perhaps telling yourself that you need a treat? Do you feel you deserve a bit of spoiling because you're depressed or angry? Have you written off the possibility of ever achieving an acceptable weight again because it seems such a long haul to get there? Does any form of exercise seem impossible to fit in because of your long working hours, dealing with the kids and having precious little time for yourself without adding another chore (exercise) to all the ones you have already ...? Are you being put off exercise now because you were rubbish at sport as a kid? Questioning any one of these common internal 'justifications' can help you discover a hidden choice-point for a new departure. For example, what else apart from food would give you a self-administered treat without the risk of adding to your weight?

3. Your mammoth may have hidden benefits for yourself or for others you care about.

We tend to think it's 'bad' to leave things undone if we believe we should be doing them. But suppose for a moment there's a benefit to *not* doing them? Sometimes, it's obvious what you might gain by not tackling your mammoth – for example, leaving the ironing for another day (or week, or even longer) probably allows you to relax or do more interesting things. Often, though, there's a hidden benefit too, and it helps to ask what *not* doing something actually achieves for you. Here are some everyday examples:

- Not clearing your desk, not doing your filing or not sorting your emails may help you avoid the uncomfortable recognition that you are a less systematic worker than you would like to be.
- Not replying to an invitation from someone may tell you that really you'd rather not accept it – the positive benefit, in the short term, is that you don't actually face saying no and risk hurting the other person's feelings.
- Not saying no to that lunchtime pizza when one of the other guys goes out to get it, and asking for a salad instead, may mean that you are not endlessly ribbed by the others for being a health junky or a goody-goody.

Once you have unearthed the hidden benefit of avoiding your mammoth, your next job is to take a good look at it, seeing it as it might appear to a curious observer from outside the situation. Challenge your own thinking. Here are some ways of challenging the examples I've just given.

- Might you be setting yourself an unrealistic standard of efficiency/neatness in regard to the state of your desk-work? How might you determine a 'good-enough' level?
- Might your friend be less hurt by a refusal of her invitation in good time and with an acceptable reason ('Actually, it's really not the kind of thing I enjoy'), than by an embarrassed excuse at the last minute?
- Is it really so bad to stand out from the crowd at work if it means you start to be healthier, more alert and better able to do your job as a result?

TRY THIS:

Think about your mammoth. Test out just how you are currently bolstering its existence by imagining that you need to convince someone else that having it delivers real benefits. Brainstorm as to what those benefits might be. Be quick. Don't try to be logical. Somewhere on your emerging list you may well find the pay-off that's working for you. The chances are that as it pops into your head or takes form at the end of your pen, you'll have a feeling of familiarity – it's an old friend/enemy, after all. If the pay-off it delivers is really significant, is there another way you can still achieve it without feeding your mammoth?

Sometimes, what's invested in keeping an old pattern alive is that the status quo also benefits other people who are important to you. When you assume that your boss, your partner or your children will object to you mastering your mammoth because it will show another side of you and turn you into a different person from the one they know, you may well be right.

- Someone who takes a degree as a mature adult, qualifies in a new profession or risks going for a promotion that will involve longer working hours and more responsibility, for example, may indeed threaten the partner who knew them as less qualified, less confident, more available or even more dependent.
- If you don't eat sensibly and remain overweight, you may not have to buy a whole new wardrobe, and could prevent competitive relatives or friends sniping at you for outdoing them in attractiveness.
- You may have stayed in the same role for ages without asking for promotion because your boss really seems to appreciate you – and that could suit your boss just fine because you are always so useful to her!
- You may find that when you try to slim down, your partner, friends or family subtly undermine your attempts. Often, these others feel threatened by any positive changes in you that might result – improved appearance or new energy, for example. So long as this pay-off remains hidden, the secret sabotage will continue and change will remain unlikely.
- If you have always been the reliable rock in a team, friendship group or relationship, you may grow to feel resentful that you are taken for granted or that you are unable to explore your more adventurous side. Breaking out of this role is a mammoth that can seem impossible to manage.

When people hang on to habits, it's often because of the fear of what change may bring and the thought of discussing the issue openly can, in itself, be daunting. It may take courage to discuss your fears with people you think may be benefiting from leaving your mammoth untamed, but doing so has some important benefits.

First, you may discover that your assumed 'beneficiaries' would not, in fact, mind if you were to change. Second, if they do have a real investment in keeping you as you are, you will know what you really have to deal with and be in a better position to frame appropriate strategies for dealing with them, as well as with your mammoth. And, third, if they do acknowledge some benefit from the status quo, letting them know that you really do want to change allows you to begin a more honest dialogue with them about what each of you might gain and lose as you move forward.

TRY THIS:

1. Ask yourself what you gain by keeping things as they are.
2. Find a quiet time when you can ask the other person(s) what they get out of your current way of behaving.
3. Ask them if they would be willing to explore other ways in which you could both still get the same benefits if you change. You're after shared investigation and shared solutions: you both have an investment in things as they were, and it would be good if you shared an investment in a new, and hopefully better, kind of relationship in future.

4. *You may be assuming that dealing with your mammoth will involve hostility or conflict.*

We all make assumptions – it can be a useful way of simplifying life, so that we can act quickly without thinking about things in detail. But we need to examine our assumptions from time to time, as it may be that they are incorrect and, as such, providing the wrong guidance.

Not allowing yourself a voice – holding back from saying what you feel for fear of others' opinions – can become a painful and debilitating mammoth and one that's usually made up of many single opportunities not taken. Have you ever:

- Not told someone they were doing something wrong because you thought they would get angry, aggressive or think ill of you?
- Not said what you really thought in a discussion at work because you thought you'd be a lone voice, or because you didn't want it to appear as though you were showing off your expertise or going above your role and status?

TRY THIS:

- Ask yourself what's preventing you from being open with the other person – for example, the colleague who promised to help you, then 'forgot'. You may be thinking, 'You're rude/inattentive/don't seem to care,' and you may well be right in assuming that just blurting this out would upset or anger them. So it's ▶

probably best to avoid a direct attack on their behaviour. You could bypass the issue of rudeness and ask for their help directly, perhaps by saying something like: 'I wonder if you could spare a moment – or shall I come back to you later when you're less busy?' (Note: your tone needs to be neutral here, not sarcastic!)

- Cover the possibility you fear by articulating it. (Self-awareness is usually disarming.) 'I may be a lone voice here, but I think we may have left out something important and I'd feel much more comfortable if it was out on the table.' Or: 'I realise I'm just here to take the minutes, but in listening to the discussion as a sort of outsider, something I've heard implied very strongly several times but not actually said out loud is ...'

5. *Not dealing with your mammoth may seem a better option than trying and failing.*

Sometimes people unconsciously sabotage their own chances of managing their mammoth because they fear they won't be able to do it well enough, or even at all. Leaving essential tasks to the last moment can give you the excuse that you'd have done better if only you'd had more time, thus relieving you of the fear that even with more time you might not have done the job as well as you wanted or hoped.

TRY THIS:

1. Ask yourself what your real issue is. Put it into words: 'I'm afraid I won't do a good enough job,' for example. Or, if you are acknowledging a bereavement, 'I can't find the right words to say how sorry I am and how much he will be missed.'

2. Ask yourself if it's really better to be thought of as someone whose work is always last-minute and rushed than as someone who made a wholehearted attempt at it. Remind yourself that where your work has honest limitations, any criticism will be more accurately related to its (and your) quality, giving you more opportunity to learn and improve.

   Express those condolences in any way that comes to you because the bereaved person would rather have your sympathy, however inadequately expressed, than think you didn't care.

6. Your mammoth may involve implicit trade-offs, rather than clear-cut agreements with others.

One of the most common, everyday interpersonal mammoths involves agreements with others that just aren't working out. How does that become a mammoth? Because usually we know we should say something, but we don't, because we fear unpleasantness or conflict if we do. Exchanges involving trade-offs or informal deals are rarely spelled out clearly, so often it's not obvious what is being exchanged for what, still less what the 'penalties' might be for attempting to confront the other person with not performing their part of the 'contract', or for asking to change the deal entirely.

For example, 'I'll take your kids to school on Mondays, if you have mine after school on Thursdays' is a clear agreement, but the following ones are much less so: 'She said she'd help with transport if we did the cakes' or, 'I put hours into checking that paper of his, but when I asked him to deputise at that important meeting when I had the flu, he said he couldn't spare the time.' These examples of contractual exchanges were virtually set up to fail because they were never clearly stated in the first place – a vague sense of 'he/she owes me' does not constitute an effective contract.

Often, the person who feels they are the loser in the exchange also believes they can't get the issue out in the open because they fear upsetting the whole apple cart of social obligations and connections in which it is enmeshed: will criticising the other mum mean she never offers you lifts again? Or that she stops her kids seeing yours? What about that weekend away you hoped she'd cover for you in exchange for helping her with the school barbecue? What about that shared camping holiday? If you take your work colleague to task, will that make him decide to drop out of that off-site meeting where his expertise could really come in useful? Will the incident be misrepresented to your boss as an example of you trying to palm some of your work off on someone else, and will it work against you when it comes to that promotion you were hoping for?

Some small businesses seem to run (or stagger along)

with many such implied contracts built in. Offering family members discounts or goods in exchange for part-time help may seem a natural deal – but what goods, in what amount and for how many hours of help? And what happens if either party feels the other is short-changing them?

TRY THIS:

1. Spell out for yourself – preferably in writing – what you think the exchange (actual or planned) actually involves.

2. If you feel it is failing, and you are the injured party, ask yourself honestly whether the other person might have understood the arrangement differently. If you are being accused of being in the wrong, ask how the misunderstanding might have come about. What were you assuming? What were they assuming? What was left unclear, and is that what has now turned out to be the bone of contention between you? Just what was said, and what wasn't, when the 'contract' was first talked about?

3. Once you are clear about what you think is involved, you can, in your own time, get your courage together and show the other person your written understanding of the contract. If you want the arrangement to continue, say so, and ask them to help you work out safeguards that will help both of you manage it better in future. Be specific. Avoid abstract words and phrases like 'reliable', 'regular', 'supportive'. What would someone actually have to do, and not do, to ▶

demonstrate their reliability as far as you are concerned? How often and for how long would someone have to do something for it to be 'regular' in your view – and in theirs? Aim for clarity about the details.

4. Write down the new arrangement – regardless of who else is involved and how informal the relationship is between you. Ask them if that's how they see it too. If not, what are the discrepancies?

5. Talk about what happens if either of you lets the other down. For example, 'If you pull out at the last moment you'll have to pay your share none the less' or 'order a taxi instead' or 'persuade one of the others to do the draft minutes, if you think you won't have time'.

Respect whatever is blocking you and investigate it fully: it can give you just the information you need to move forward.

Finding out what stops you dealing with your mammoth involves honest – sometimes even uncomfortable – conversations with yourself. Only this will give you a firm footing from which to move forward personally or negotiate with others. Unwrapping the layers of assumptions, self-doubts and misunderstanding that often clothe your mammoth without your realising it can, in itself, start to make it seem smaller and more amenable. Once you've successfully pinpointed what's been stopping you managing your mammoth, you'll be in a good place to assess the personal strengths and style you bring to the job of working with it. And I'm going to explore that in the next chapter.

3

What Kind of Mammoth-tamer Are You?

Now you know what has been preventing you from managing your mammoth, you are in a better position to make a start. But there are many different ways of successfully managing mammoths: what's going to be *your* way?

In this chapter, I'm going to talk about two key features of your personal style – your energy and the size of task or issue you naturally feel comfortable in handling. Each has important effects on the way you think about your mammoth and how you go about managing it.

1. *The kind of energy you have over a particular time span.*

The CEO of a highly successful company asked a coach to help him with succession planning as he wanted to spend less time at work, while still ensuring that the company was well managed and able to continue developing. In addition to their one-to-one conversations, the coach spent time shadowing the CEO to see exactly how he went about things and to get an idea of what the company would lose as he began to pull back from his active role. It became clear that the CEO's greatest strengths lay in his feel for moment-by-moment interactions and his rapid, intuitive grasp of opportunities and ideas: this was one reason why he found succession planning so difficult. In action, he was largely a 'sprinter': he really didn't have any specific long-term goals for the company, and relied mostly on colleagues to provide middle-term strategies.

2. *The way you approach problems in your mind: do you first think of the detail or of the bigger picture?*

A client of mine, a financial director in the NHS, thought one of her team members was underperforming – he seemed unable to keep overall goals in focus and kept getting 'lost in detail'. Only when she explored the issue of natural big- and small-chunk preferences did my client realise that she had been expecting a detail person to adopt a big-picture overview. 'No wonder he's having problems,' she said.

The mammoth that began this book

The idea for this book arose when my husband Leo and I faced a mammoth of our own: clearing the garage.

'Let's put two or three days aside in the diary to get it done,' Leo kept saying. And each time I heard the words 'two or three days' my heart sank. At first, I avoided replying. Then I said I couldn't spare that amount of time.

When I thought about it, I realised that while Leo likes working away at something consistently, even if it takes him a while, I prefer working in short, sharp bursts. As a young man, Leo was a middle-distance runner: he had good stamina, but little variety of speed. By contrast, I tend to go full-tilt at whatever I do, but quickly run out of energy. How were we going to manage working together? Eventually, I said: 'I can't bear the idea of committing to this for any length of time, but I'll give it twenty minutes – right now!'

This gave us a structure that was actually successful. In fact, the sessions were usually longer than my twenty-minute allowance, but the concept of bite-sizing helped us realise that if we were to work together effectively, we had to do it in short, sharp bursts. As a team, we possessed different kinds of energy and time spans. Leo had more reserves of stamina, while I had higher drive and energy. It wasn't that one approach was inherently 'better' or 'worse': we simply needed to 'cut our coat according to our cloth'.

Do the best with what's available.

Accordingly, we identified smallish, manageable tasks we could do in a short time, each of which contributed to the larger aim of getting the garage clear. Sorting out the boots, the tools, dealing with the plastic-bag mountain, the riding gear, the spare electrical stuff … you get the idea. Some things were discarded and went to the tip, others were given away – the principle was to fill the car boot and get rid of it as quickly as possible. Each load we tipped or took to a charity shop gave us an instant reward. Rewards are important. If you are breaking your mammoth down into bite-sized portions, each one must give you a flavour of success.

We used the same method not long after this when we decided to paint the kitchen. The large-chunk approach that comes naturally to Leo would have involved clearing everything out – not just furniture and functional equipment, but decorative ornaments on walls and shelves, as well as on bench-surfaces. My heart sank at the very idea. What did seem manageable to me was my smaller bite-sized approach of clearing everything on or near one wall at a time, together with its corresponding section of ceiling, and painting that. As a result, it only took us a few stress-free sessions to get everything painted, tidied and refreshed.

Using your natural style to best effect

Once you recognise what *your* style is and the way it works, you are in a better position to make the most of it and to try to ensure that you can contribute most effectively to accomplishing mammoth tasks and achieving mammoth goals, whether at work or at home. Equally, if you recognise and appreciate someone else's style when it differs from yours, you will find it easier to work with them on mammoths you face together.

Think for a moment about actual animal trainers. They are not all alike, even though they are in the same business. There may be some key things most of them have in common (for example, firmness of purpose and clarity in communicating) and others they all have to do (such as make a connection with the animal being tamed and create a relationship that has clear roles and expectations), but there will also be significant differences between them. Some tamers are flamboyant, others hold back from parading their ego; some are dominant, some more ready to negotiate; some are gentler, some harsher. Such differences in approach relate to the tamers' personalities and preferred styles. There is a difference between the *processes* involved in connecting to and taming a powerful animal and the tamer's individual *style* of carrying out those processes. You shouldn't be trying to turn yourself into something you are not: going 'against your grain' like that would add to your difficulties and almost certainly be unsuccessful.

Your 'best distance'

If you were a runner, would you be best at sprints or long distances? Even if you do not actually run, think about the *energy* you put into the things that you do, and how much *stamina* you have.

Some people naturally pace themselves to continue what they are doing for hours at a time. These are the world's *long-distancers*. In dealing with a mammoth task, they are not put off by how long it might take, and they will usually go at it with moderate but sustainable energy. Even if their slow-but-sure way of doing things causes impatience in family or colleagues, they usually get there in the end. Others (the *middle-distancers*) are more flexible in managing both speed and stamina: they are multi-paced, mixing patches of moderate tempo and energy with quicker, more dynamic, bursts of attack and finish where needed. Yet others are *sprinters*: they work best in short bursts with high energy and mental drive over short periods of time. The downside of this is that not all tasks can be done in one go or at high speed.

We can all learn from each other, and adapt our style to a certain extent; but we will find it easiest working 'our way'. Complex tasks involving teams and organisations are likely to need a mix of different approaches, but all too often managers think about allocating tasks to people with different qualifications and experience, rather than taking into account how they naturally go about things.

What happens when the tamer doesn't think about their natural style when approaching their particular mammoth? My friend Jan Pye, who is also a coach, happened to phone an acquaintance who was busy preparing for the arrival of visitors. In addition to tidying up and making beds, she'd set herself the job of cleaning all the windows. 'You've got a long-distance task there,' Jan said. 'But are you a long-distance person?' There was a pause, then the reply: 'I suppose not. Actually, I'm more of a sprinter type.'

In order to better harmonise the other woman's approach with the mammoth task she had set herself (she was determined to do it), Jan suggested that she tackle the windows one room at a time, with changes of activity in between, both to provide new interest and help her to recover energy. In this way, Jan showed her a way of managing this particular mammoth that went with, rather than against, her natural style.

By definition, mammoth tasks and projects seem huge to the person undertaking them: magnitude won't daunt a natural long-distancer as much as a sprinter, but it's possible that a long-distancer may spend more time than they actually need to in getting the job done, simply because they are used to working slowly and carefully. A sprinter approaching their own particular mammoth can easily be discouraged when they run out of time, steam or interest in the job, and may give up, when a more varied series of punchy attempts would have allowed them to succeed.

There really is no such thing as a perfect approach.

Sprinters, middle- and long-distancers can all use their natural skills to manage mammoths effectively – but not all natural approaches work with all mammoths. By recognising what your natural style is, you can begin to discover how effective it can be with your particular mammoth. If the fit isn't quite right, you will have a better idea of the help you need and whom to ask for it.

For example, one of the decisions the CEO (see pp. 33–4) realised he'd already made was to include some middle- and long-distancers in his senior team. He knew intuitively what was missing. They complemented his sprinter's decisive ability with their longer-term strategic views. In taking on a coach, he was again following his gut instinct and effectively acquiring an even longer-distance perspective.

For my client the finance director, appreciating the

lack of 'fit' between her team member and his task was the start of a team shuffle that made better use of several people's aptitudes.

If you are working alone, you might consider talking through an issue, task or problem with a colleague, friend or family member who would be able to supply you with a different perspective and help you find a new way of thinking about it or a more effective strategy for taking things forward.

TRY THIS:

Diagnostic: what's your best distance?

- Are you someone who gets easily bored?
- Do you enjoy skipping from one thing to another?
- Do you enjoy doing things like housework or gardening in a random way, with one thing leading you on to another just because it happens to be in the place where you finished up the last bit?
- Do you find it hard to take a middle-distance view and imagine what you'll be doing more than two or three years from now?
- Do you find it difficult to take a long-distance perspective and imagine what or where you'll be five or ten years from now?
- Do you tend to get impatient with people who think or act more slowly than you do?
- Do you have high energy that soon peters out?

▶

If you've answered 'Yes' to a number of these, you're probably a *sprinter*, and you'll be more successful if you break your task down into sprints you can tackle one by one.

- Do you get satisfaction out of focusing at work on one thing at a time?
- Do you get irritated when you're interrupted in the middle of something?
- Are you comfortable making and sticking to long-term plans?
- Would you pride yourself on being slow, but sure?
- Do you tend to think that people who do things quickly are probably slapdash?
- Do you find it natural to think and plan long term – ten or more years ahead?
- Can you keep going at something for a relatively long time?
- Do you find it difficult to speed up for emergencies or short deadlines?

If you've answered 'Yes' to a number of these, you're probably a long-distancer, and you'll need to manage the conditions around you so as to allow yourself enough time and space to get stuck in and make good progress.

- Can you vary your pace of attack without too much difficulty when you have to?
- Do you like to start something slowly and carefully ▶

and only speed up once you've got into your rhythm or
are near the end?

- Once you've set your pace, can you sustain it?
- Would you be comfortable planning five to ten years
  ahead?
- Can you manage tasks with different time spans and
  degrees of urgency at the same time?

If you've answered 'Yes' to a number of these, you may
be a middle-distancer. You may have some advantages
here because you can adapt, but this flexibility may
sometimes mean you lose focus, energy and drive if other
demands are being made on you.

Your natural chunk or bite size

The phrase 'biting off more than one can chew' reminds us
of what we all know – that breaking things down into
chunks is a fact of life. You can only deal with so much at a
time, whether it's a project, a burden or a volume of information. The phrase 'sound-bite' relates to this too: a
sound-bite is a pithy summary which relies on brevity and
conciseness to reach a wide audience via the media. If the
bite of information were too big, its impact would be lost.

Chunk size isn't simply to do with the volume of information, but rather to do with its degree of generalisation or
detail. Just as everyone has their natural 'distance', so each
of us also has our preferred chunk size: some people like to
get the big picture first, or even to work largely with an

overview, while others are more comfortable starting with the detail or, indeed, perhaps remaining with it. These natural preferences need taking into account when you are faced with a mammoth, whatever it may involve.

Your chunking preferences combine with your available energy and stamina in individual ways. There isn't a simple equation or pairing between distance and chunk size, but rather a more subtle interplay of approach and focus.

One young woman we know was interested in animals from early childhood and always wanted to be a vet – a long-term project that involved getting GCSE exam qualifications, A levels, doing work placements at farms and veterinary surgeries during school-holiday times and a commitment to years of college study and professional placements. What sustained her throughout was the belief that she could – and would – eventually build a career for a lifetime. She was a long-distancer whose large-chunk view of her future helped her to manage the small-chunk hurdles she had to clear in order to achieve her overall ambition.

Someone with a sprinter's approach could actually achieve much the same things as she did in the end, but would probably be seeing the obstacles on the route to their mammoth project as separate building blocks to be dealt with one by one.

When I set out to write my D. Phil thesis I felt intimidated by the thought of having to write 80,000 words about the fieldwork I'd done and the interviews I'd conducted with approximately ninety people over eighteen months. It seemed too much to manage and too long a time frame to contemplate. In the end, I managed it by breaking it down into the short, sharp chunks I could handle, which meant making a plan, then setting a target on a week-by-week basis. That felt much more my style, and I was able to do it.

What's worked best for you in the past?

It's likely that as you've been reading this, you'll have recognised yourself as either a big-picture, large-chunk person or as a detail, small-chunk one. Experiences at school, at work and in your home life could all have provided you with examples. Maybe you'll also have gained a sense of some of the advantages and disadvantages of each approach.

Your natural chunk-size preference will affect how you view your mammoth initially – either as a hulking great entity (big-chunk, whole) or as a series of things to do, obstacles to surmount or hurdles to clear (small-chunk, detailed view). Successfully managing a mammoth requires you to combine the two: you will need to develop a big picture of what you want to achieve and to create a detailed strategy for getting there and this book will help you do that.

Now you can do a reality check by trawling through some of your past history of mammoth-managing – the times it worked and the times it didn't. Testing out the descriptions I've given against the reality of your experience can help you think more deeply about yourself – and others – and show you where further explorations or conversations would help you fill in more detail or answer questions that puzzle you.

So in the light of what you now know, what can you take forward from your past mammoth-managing experience to help you in future? For example, what part did your energy, stamina and natural chunk size each play in how you got on?

Mammoth-managing in teams

Managing your mammoth in your own style is not so difficult when you are working independently, but what about those times when you have to work alongside others whose style differs from yours? This can happen at home or at work. Often, work groups are referred to as teams, but the reality may be that the members are working *in parallel*, not that they are working *together*.

> **A true team is a group whose members are dovetailing their skills and natural bite sizes to work towards the same project or task (mammoth).**

The trick to good teamwork – and remember that families and friendship groups can also be teams – is to make the most of the different styles and approaches of each member and draw on the best of their natural styles to help with the job you're involved in together. If you are a manager, try to work out the features of your colleagues' personal styles, and place them where they can use them to everyone's best advantage. Sprinters will be good at spearheading new projects, giving ones that are long-drawn-out a needed boost at times as they go along, and helping to whip everything together towards the end. Middle-distancers can be very useful throughout a big project because of their flexibility. Long-distancers will stay the course at a steady, unflagging pace.

Talk openly with the team members about the advantages of their different approaches. Put each kind of stylist where they can work to their strengths. Try to help them understand the qualities they can bring to the project and to appreciate the value of approaches that differ from their own. That way, you'll acknowledge everyone, cut down on impatience about the way other people go about things and generate more co-operation. Whether your mammoth is planning and enjoying a family holiday, setting up a new system at work, completing a project or increasing your department's effectiveness, working as a stylish team at taming it will be quicker, more harmonious and, ultimately, more successful.

TRY THIS:

Even if your project is a relatively small and everyday one (for example, sorting out what you and the other members of your family want to do this weekend and how you are going to fit it all in, or planning a meeting at work), try starting by saying something like: 'Now you've got lots of

▶

stamina, so why don't you do X, and as I'm more of a short-sharp-burst person, I'll tackle this bit and then that bit, and we can check progress a bit later.'

The more you and the others in your team get used to thinking like this when tackling smaller mammoths, the easier you'll all find it when you have to face a large one together.

Thinking about the nature of your mammoth, the kind of things that up till now have stopped you managing it and your own characteristic approaches as a mammoth-tamer has given you a solid foundation for making a start.

One of the things that NLP has taught us is that effective people in any sphere of life tend to use similar strategies for doing what they do. So you won't be surprised to learn that though mammoths vary greatly in their nature, we don't need to invent specialised ways to cope with different sorts. The next chapter introduces you to a mammoth-manager's tool-kit which will help you with any and every kind of mammoth that may cross your path.

4

Sure and Simple Strategies for Mammoth-managers

You may have come across the acronym KISS; it stands for *Keep it simple stupid* and was invented by the lead engineer at the pioneering aerospace firm Lockheed Martin as a way of guiding his designers. He wanted them to remember two key things: firstly, that the planes they were designing would, like all machines, at some point inevitably break down; and secondly, that when this happened they would have to be fixed by ordinary mechanics with basic tools. Simplicity in design was therefore the recipe for success. (And by the way, 'stupid' wasn't what he was calling his staff: it was a way of telling them that their designs needed to be 'no-brainers'.)

Simple is better because there's less to go wrong, and if it does go wrong, it's easier to work out what the problem is. And simple directions or principles are also easier to remember.

Managing mammoths is a tough enough task – you know, because you've already tried it – without having to remember and follow a complicated set of instructions. So while various chapters of this book show you how to approach different kinds of mammoth, this chapter brings together a simple set of guidelines that underlie managing *all* kinds of mammoth. They're organised into three groupings:

- Your baseline
- Your thinking
- Your tactics.

Your baseline

Before you take your first step towards managing your mammoth, you need to know exactly how you are placed right here and right now. Establishing just what's causing you problems, assessing the resources you can bring to bear and working out in advance possible tactics that could help you achieve greater mastery help you build a sure overall strategy and, at the same time, allow you to monitor the changes that will provide evidence of your progress.

> **Time spent in reconnaissance is never wasted.**

Face the facts

If, like one of my banking clients, you're in a mess, the starting point is something like my first words to him: 'OK, you're in the shit. Now how do we get you out?'

Where you are, even if it seems bleak at the moment, is

actually your surest starting point for getting your mammoth under control. It can be worth your while to take a good look at your current situation in detail – making changes at the level of small but significant detail is do-able, economical of effort and often enough to set off a 'cascade' effect of changes that roll you in the right direction. Try to put feelings of inadequacy and emotions like blame and guilt about your unmanaged mammoth to one side. Your energies are best used now for the way forward.

Refresh your vision – what do you really want?

Have clear in your mind what managing your mammoth would be like. Whether you're going to get into a cut-down process or a build-up one, you really need to know where you're headed. Any arguments with yourself that come up at this point can provide potentially useful information (see Chapter 2: What Stops You Managing It?) and should be registered and treated as such. Do not let them alter the way you frame your vision and your goal, just take them as additional information.

Make your vision of achievement as detailed and specific as you can. For example, 'Losing a pound of weight a week until I reach my final target' provides you with a clearer goal than just 'losing weight', and because it's specific it gives you a better way to measure your progress and recognise eventual success.

A client of mine involved in NHS financial planning and accounting was not a natural networker, but knew that she needed to build better links both in-house and within the area covered by the Trust she worked for, if she was to improve the system. To make it work better, she knew she'd need the closer collaboration of colleagues in other departments and allied local organisations, and she knew what this would involve in quite specific detail. On the basis of our discussions, she drew on her experience of having lived in a village for many years to help her tap into existing professional networks and create new ones. To her surprise, she found colleagues much more ready than she'd expected to offer the information, advice and support she needed. In the process, she discovered she was a good networker after all!

Know why you want to make changes

What's your rationale for change? A wish, an intent, a belief that things can be different is your platform for exerting leverage on how things are at present. Just establishing what that rationale is, is the first step out of the mammoth-dominated place you have been stuck in up till now. Statements like, 'Things can't go on this way' or, 'I/We deserve better' or, 'This is preventing me from doing what I know I'm meant to do' can help you articulate just what your personal platform is. And the clearer your platform is to you, the firmer and stronger a base it offers to support the changes you are working on.

A client of mine set herself the task of learning a set of very complex and sophisticated riding skills and teaching them to her horse – a mammoth process that involved months of dedicated work retraining their musculature and refining their ways of communicating with each other. What was her platform? It was her belief that it would help them both through times when her horse, who suffered from recurrent lameness, was slowly recovering and could only be allowed to exercise at walk. Each episode of limited exercise lasted over a month, and both of them had been getting bored and frustrated. My client wanted to keep their minds alert and, at the same time, help them both become more supple.

Remember, less is often more

This phrase has almost become a cliché now, but it's profound none the less. And it doesn't mean you should be satisfied with any old intervention so long as it's a small one. *Less is more when it's properly targeted.* Michelangelo said that the sculptor's task is to remove every bit of a block of stone that is *not* essential to the statue locked inside it. A similar idea underpins Occam's razor, a principle in logical thought that says one good argument will be enough in itself: it doesn't need backing up with six others. In other words, don't try to do with more what can be done with less. In managing your mammoth, aim for crisp, straightforward economy of thought and action.

One of my clients went for this strategy when his boss asked him to take on yet another piece of work. He could have said how overworked he was already. He could have suggested someone else be given the work instead. He could have asked how short the deadline was, or even asked for extra time. Instead, he said simply: 'Yes, I can do that. What do you want me to drop instead?'

A simple action can be enough to start wheels turning

You may have heard the proverb, 'For want of a nail the shoe was lost' which describes a situation where the loss of one nail ultimately led to the loss of a kingdom.

This chaining of consequences works both ways. Make a first start on repairing something that's gone wrong, and you create the possibility not just for stopping the rot, but for turning a disaster into something acceptable or even good. Stand your ground with a colleague or boss who is bullying you and you introduce a doubt into their minds about how much or for how long they can continue to behave like this. Change a long-standing habit by identifying a single difference you can go on repeating until it creates the new habit you're seeking.

Sarah found it difficult to manage her finances. She started to take control of them one day by the single, simple action of drawing enough cash from the bank to cover her estimated spending for one week and refusing to let herself spend any more in the following seven days. Of course, there was more to do, but she had made a start on the mammoth – and hitherto unachievable – task of changing her relationship with money. By taking that one initial action that was different from those that had locked her into financial inadequacy up till then, she set off a chain of reactions. One difference created other possibilities, and working with those put her in the business of becoming an effective money-manager in the future.

A change at a relatively insignificant level of activity can often be enough to alter things at higher levels

This point is a slightly more sophisticated application of the 'less is more' principle, in that it gets us thinking about the effects that *different kinds of small intervention* can have. Robert Dilts, who is one of the outstanding theorists and practitioners of NLP, developed a hierarchy of concepts known as the Neurological Levels. Between them, these six concepts cover every aspect of our lives, from things like the plumbing or the phone bill (Environment), via what we do (Behaviour), our knowledge and skills (Capabilities), our Beliefs and Values and our sense of Identity, to our highest sense of Mission or Purpose in life. By and large, most of us would agree that material things and arrangements (environment) are somehow less important than 'higher-level' matters of belief, identity and purpose, but they can act as powerful levers on those higher levels none the less.

Often, mammoths do arise around higher-level issues, but even when they do, you don't have to start at the top. You are much more likely to succeed if you start by changing something lower down.

A recent television programme about buildings and their effect featured an office block which included many small rooms and spaces where staff could freely go to meet, to think or to see clients. The layout of some of these was conventional, while others were more quirkily designed and furnished. The message that this environment conveyed wasn't just one of physical variety, comfort and degrees of formality and informality. It operated at a much higher level – the building told the employees: your comfort of mind and body matters; we're not going to watch over and clock you in and out because we trust you to make the best use of your time; you know what conditions help you work at your best; you can choose.

When you personally 'go the extra mile' (be it literally or metaphorically) by doing something practical for someone, whether it's a colleague, a friend or a family member, you are telling them that *they matter.* Your (relatively low-level) *behaviour* towards them has affected them at the high level of *identity*.

Interrupt the current pattern

Patterns become automatic: if you are to spot possible choice-points for doing something different, you need first to identify and then interrupt the pattern involved. In Chapter 2, I explained how patterns involve choice-points that have become invisible through familiarity. You can change a pattern by taking a new option at a choice-point you've identified. Or you can make a change at random anywhere in the pattern – because any change opens up new possibilities. *The Dice Man*, a fascinating novel published in 1971, was built around this theory: it concerned a man who decided that he would make choices by assigning possible options a number from 1 to 6 and then throw a die and take the option that came up. This strategy is rather extreme – but it makes the point that you can only go in a new direction if you do something *different*!

Here are some simple examples of pattern-interrupts:

- If you always reach for something sweet at your tea-break, break the pattern by putting the biscuits in an unexpected place. You could try locking them in the garage. You may still end up eating that biscuit – but you will have to make an active, not an automatic, unthinking, choice to do so.
- If you have been putting off sending an email or making a phone call, put the recipient's name on today's shopping list or stick it to the kettle.
- If your desk is awash with paperwork, put your wastepaper basket on top of your desk so that its little open mouth just pleads with you to feed it.

Be inventive. Be funny. Be outrageous. Finding something outlandish like a shoe or a hammer in your fridge will catch your attention and make you think about what you were reaching in for, and whether you really have to have it after all.

Pattern-interrupts can be effective in themselves because they make you aware of something you have learned to ignore. Use them to highlight an immediate choice, or to help build a better or less damaging habit (for more on this, see Chapter 8).

I bit my nails until I was forty. As a child, no amount of scolding, bribery or even tincture of bitter aloes painted on my unsightly stumps had any effect. Through hypnosis, when I was eventually helped to give up, the substitute that actually worked was wearing chunky necklaces. The therapist helped me generate a harmless substitute activity that replaced the damaging one: whenever I was thinking or reading (my automatic nibbling times), my fingers would brush the beads on their way up to my mouth and would find a chance to fiddle in a different way.

Your thinking

Mammoths can exist in their own right; but we can also create ones where none exists, make small ones larger or big ones smaller by the way we think about them.

> **Becoming aware of the part your thinking plays in your mammoth is a key step towards managing it more effectively.**

Begin with what seems easiest

Earlier in the book, I explained that some of our taken-for-granted thinking about mammoths makes them seem harder to deal with and may not actually have a basis in fact (see pp. 6–7). Often, we assume that getting to grips with a mammoth we find huge and difficult to deal with will be a task that's just as huge and difficult, and this may prevent us looking for small interventions that could make real differences (see the 'Less is more' point above). Allow yourself to make what seems the easiest change – as far as *you* are concerned. (There is rarely any mileage in taking on the biggest, hardest, challenge you can envisage!) Starting your mammoth-managing with something that appears easy is not a 'cop out'. In fact, it has a number of real benefits:

- You'll start sooner, so you'll feel relieved and more decisive.
- You can do what's needed quicker, so you'll have more time for everything else in your life.
- It will seem like less effort, so you'll be encouraged to become a long-term mammoth-manager.
- You'll feel you're in charge of yourself, even if not yet of your mammoth, simply because you've made a start – and that sets off a positive spiral of energy and activity.

Taking control of personal habits – such as eating, drinking or smoking – is a common example. Deal with one drink at a time, one day at a time is the AA watchword, and it really works. It's the difference between saying to yourself: *I did what I set out to do today* and *I achieved 5 per cent of my target today*.

Changing the balance of power in a relationship at home or work can also start with something small.

One of my clients felt she was being ignored in meetings, even when she had something useful or important to say.

Since the only person she could change was herself, what could she do to tip the balance?

We looked at several low-level possibilities: did she dress 'visibly' or 'invisibly' at work? Did she sit where she could catch the chairperson's attention? We established that because she felt uncomfortable and expected to be ignored, she'd often arrive close to a meeting's start time, when the only seats left were at the back of the group or outside the main circle. So for the next meeting, where she really wanted her views heard, she brightened up her usual grey outfit with a bright turquoise scarf and made a point of arriving in good time, so she could get a seat directly opposite the chairperson. The flash of bright colour when she leaned forward to speak meant that she automatically attracted the chair's attention and created the opening she needed.

Be as inquisitive about consequences as about causes

It's easy to assume that you need to discover how your unmanageable mammoth came into your life – psychological theory and therapies place great emphasis on the history of problems, and our current 'blame culture' tends to focus on why things went wrong and who was responsible. Newsreaders and spokespersons often talk about lessons having been learned – as if that's enough in itself. But what will you (or anyone) do differently next time as a result of that learning?

We all need to become more aware of the possible

consequences of our actions and those of others, and more imaginative about ways of dealing with them. Systems theory, the interdisciplinary study of how all kinds of complex organisations whether physical (human body), social (businesses, societies and groups) or mechanical (machines and assembly lines), tells us that any action in the system will lead to further actions and reactions. Here's an organisational example where one change in a corporation has unexpected knock-on effects in other departments or on sales figures.

> Geoff managed a team of about ten people in a large open-plan office where people sat facing each other in long rows of workstations, separated only by computer screens. Geoff told me that he got on more easily with some of his team than with others, and found it easier to manage them. Where did the ones he felt more distant from sit? In the next bank of desks! Since so many people were involved it wasn't practical to alter the team's seating arrangements. However, Geoff could make a point of getting up and talking directly with the other team members in person, rather than relying on phoning or even emailing them as he did at present. After a few weeks of this, he reported that he now felt much more connected to the 'distant' team members, and they too had started walking across to talk not only with him but with other colleagues.

Systems aren't just organisational entities: an individual human being is made up of interlocking systems, in which physical, mental and emotional 'happenings' all have effects on each other, creating an almost seamless web of cause and effect. Because of this connectedness, something that happens anywhere within that personal system will inevitably have consequences elsewhere. Thinking is an activity that involves your body's internal communications and its physiology: thinking has systemic effects internally which can, in turn, lead to systemic effects externally. Your thinking creates what you are doing, and your doing has effects on the social systems of which you're part. That's why changing your thinking can often start a cascade of much broader changes.

If you don't get the result you hope for, change the way you're thinking

The old adage 'If at first you don't succeed, try, try, and try again' is not a good one to go by. Einstein said: 'We cannot solve our problems with the same thinking we used when we created them.' By all means, repeat an approach or strategy once, perhaps even twice, to check you have done your best with it. But if it's still not getting you the result you're after, don't expend more time and energy on any more repetitions. What you need is a different approach.

You probably need to stop relying solely or mainly on the rational part of your brain and instead allow yourself to turn to some of your other in-built ways of thinking and problem-solving. Hypothesise. Start asking, 'What might happen if I did X instead of Y?' That way, you're more likely to tap into unconscious processes, like making new or unexpected links between things, bringing together items of information you didn't know you had (there's more about this in Chapter 13) and, as a result, come up with creative, innovative ideas that just might unstick what's stuck. But how do you go about this?

TRY THIS:

Take a few moments to stare off into space and let your mind float around the problem. 'Dream a little dream.' Or, just before you go to sleep, set yourself the overnight possibility of coming up with something you just hadn't seen as relevant – till now. Often, important reshuffling of ideas can happen outside of your awareness like this, and new approaches just 'arrive' when you wake up in the morning. Or challenge yourself by saying: if the logical approaches haven't worked, what's the most *illogical* approach?

Praise yourself for any change you make even when you know there's more work to do

In their book *How Full Is Your Bucket?*, the Gallup researchers and workplace experts Tom Rath and Donald Clifton report that people who are recognised and praised at work:

- increase productivity
- increase engagement among colleagues
- stay with their organisations
- receive better scores from customers
- have better safety records at work.

It's reasonably obvious that such interpersonal strokes and pats can have a significant impact on the receiver, and on the quality of their relationship with the person who gives them (whether their senior or equal). Less obvious, until you come to think it through, is the impact such recognition can have on you if you give it to *yourself*. If you keep changing your goal-posts, or reminding yourself how much more of your mammoth still remains, it's little wonder if such negative self-feedback depletes your energy and enthusiasm for the task you've set yourself. You don't need to be fulsome – none of the overcooked praise of 'every day and in every way I get better and better'! Be realistic. 'That was hard, or scary, but I managed to get through it.' 'Today I made a start.' 'I noticed a small but real difference in the way I felt, how she responded, or the time it took.'

Your tactics

Where strategies are our overall approaches to a problem, tactics are the specific actions we can take to put those approaches to work in an everyday context. Again, I want to stress how effective small, often unobtrusive, tactics can often be.

Less is more.

Create a new habit of continuously making small improvements

When someone is really wedded to the idea of change, they want it all as soon as possible (big chunk!). Ambition and determination provide fuel, but you can be overambitious and overdetermined. The technique now known by the Japanese name of Kaizen was invented in the Depression with the aim of getting American industry going again. Work supervisors were urged to look for as many *little* ways as possible to improve their product and the methods of its production. Workers were encouraged to report on small inefficiencies and suggest simple ways to eradicate them. After the Second World War, the same technique was introduced into Japan to help rebuild its shattered economy.

In his book *One Small Step Can Change Your Life*, Dr Robert Maurer says:

> By taking small steps, you effectively rewire your nervous system so that it does the following:
>
> - 'unsticks' you from a creative block
> - bypasses the flight-or-fight response
> - creates new connections between neurons so that the brain enthusiastically takes over the process of change and you progress rapidly toward your goal.

There are two principles at work here: one is looking out for *small* improvements. The other is keeping on looking for *even more* of them. By asking small questions and taking the smallest steps you can take towards your goal, you can also get yourself unconsciously looking out for the next question, the next step and the next improvement. And because change – which includes the managing of mammoths – is rarely a 'done deal' you will be creating a habit of making fine but continual adjustments to keep yourself on track.

Do something *today*

The hardest part about good intentions is doing something about them. This is particularly true if your goal is huge and vague: 'I want to get my mammoth under control.' That's great – but how are you going to do it? Once you have identified your first small step (see above) – do it *today*.

- Don't keep telling yourself, 'I must get in touch with old Jo again.' Instead, pick up the phone (or email if that feels less terrifying) and say, 'Hello, I'm sorry I've been out of touch for so long.'·
- Instead of saying, 'I really need to lose weight,' do something about it today – like taking half a spoonful of sugar, rather than a whole one in your next coffee or substituting dessertspoons for tablespoons of potato, rice or pasta at your next meal.
- If you have been saying for ages that you want to improve your French, buy a French magazine tonight on the way home from work and get tuned in relatively painlessly with plenty of help from pictures and adverts.

Today is always better than tomorrow: by tomorrow your new start will be a day old and will be opening up yet further possibilities ...

Repetition is what makes a change into a habit, so begin a new habit by tagging it on to an existing one

We are busy people in a busy century. When are you going to find the time to practise a new skill or learn a new habit? The easiest way is to tag the behaviour you want to become habitual on to a habit you already have. Attach your new habit to established daily routines like showering, cleaning your teeth, journeying to and from work, returning home after the school run. You always remember them. By doing your stretches, your mindfulness meditation, your power walk, your day-planning exercise, your novel reading or your mental debriefing from work in partnership with patterns that already exist in your life, you'll quickly make the new patterns habitual too.

For example, if your aim is to get reading more, why not make use of your commute to work and do as an acquaintance of my father's did. He was head of one of the national power companies during the war, and had a half-hour train journey to work and back, so used that time to teach himself languages. As he said, 'An hour spent every day on any subject quickly turns someone into an expert.' The book you decide to read on the tube tomorrow will soon be finished and probably followed by another. Soon reading could be one of your most reliable and valued habits.

Gilly had struggled unsuccessfully to make herself do her yoga, so she decided she'd listen to the television news every evening instead of watching it. That way, she could keep abreast of current affairs and do her floor exercises at the same time.

Be clear and direct with yourself and with others

When your mammoth involves other people, the simplest and most direct communication is usually the most effective. When you can, pre-plan. What is it you want to ask? What do you want to tell them? How would you like them to help you? First, be clear with yourself. Then you will find it easier to be clear with the other person, giving them a signpost that lets them know where you're headed and how you want them to be involved.

- Are you going to warn your boss now that you would like to take your annual leave in three months' time? Or will you wait till a few weeks beforehand and just hope that slot is still free?

- Are you going to make a simple, straightforward proposal to your partner or colleague? Or run the risk of losing their attention and perhaps confusing them by giving them the full explanation of the thought processes that led you to suggesting it?

- Did you do ten stretches this morning? Or aim for a full workout along with that exercise video?

- Did you clear enough space on your desk yesterday for the A4 file you're working from? Or tell yourself you really ought to get the whole desk emptied?

In each case, the first option is clear, brief and uncompli-cated, takes a relatively short time and is complete in itself – it is therefore more achievable. So that's the option to go for.

Experiment and then review what happens

Many of the world's greatest discoveries have been made through accident or experimentation. The key to creating an experimental approach is in the way you think about your 'mistakes'. You are likely to feel very differently about them if, like Thomas Edison, the world's most pro-lific inventor, you tell yourself: 'If I find 10,000 ways something won't work, I haven't failed. I am not discour-aged, because every wrong attempt discarded is another step forward.'

Try taking every 'failure' as *information*. Information is something you can use to adjust your approach or to select another one entirely. Old problems rarely get solved by old strategies, though they often do by new ones.

By now you'll have a good idea of how to identify the kind of mammoth that's looming in your life. You will know what it is that's prevented you managing it in the past. You will have a better idea of the qualities you uniquely bring to the challenge you've set yourself. And, as a result of this last chapter, you will possess a range of tried-and-tested strategies for taking on that challenge successfully.

So far, what I've said applies to virtually all mammoths. Now it's time to help you tailor your approach more specifically to the mammoth that actually confronts you. If you want to reduce an unwanted mammoth, such as a 'bad habit' or an unhelpful set of feelings, you will need to break it down. That's the subject of Section Two.

SECTION TWO

Cutting Mammoths Down to Size

5

Beyond Choredom

How do you feel about chores? Domestic and office chores can often assume mammoth size and status in our minds. We need a way to break down these everyday mammoths into manageable chunks, and we can do that not just in the way we already know – doing chores conscientiously and regularly – but by transforming the way we think of them. This chapter is going to help you explore how to do this, so you can discover for yourself the possibilities that lie beyond choredom.

Do jobs like preparing expense claims, keeping accounts, washing up, tidying and ironing represent mammoths to you? Some people hate having to cook every day. What about weeding? Or mowing the lawn? Sorting paperwork for your tax return or your work-expenses claim? Or doing your homework? When some routine home or office task looms, do you feel irritated? Overwhelmed? Despairing? And just what is it about this kind of task that gets to you? Is it the fact that it comes round again and again? Is it the low-level mindlessness of it? Is it the lack of any real sense of accomplishment? Or is it your own impatience with yourself that you haven't got around to it, that you let it get to you, or on top of you ... ? The aim of this chapter is to help you feel differently about chores in some way that will make doing them easier, more meaningful, more satisfying or perhaps even more enjoyable.

Every necessary task is a chore to someone, a bore to someone and a satisfaction to someone else. If you are someone who actually enjoys doing your chores and are wondering why you are reading this chapter, one answer is that it can help you understand the rest of us better!

It's how chores make you *feel* that matters. And that depends on how you think of them – how, in the NLP word, you 'frame' them in your head.

Not long after we married, my husband Leo and I decided to employ a cleaner: both in full-time employment, we resented spending our limited free time dusting and vacuuming. Our cleaner had a different view: she really enjoyed coming into a mildly dishevelled, mildly dirty house each week and leaving it crisp, clean and orderly. The only condition she made was that she would never work for someone who didn't themselves work. By doing what she was good at and enjoyed, she knew she was enabling someone else to do the same. That sense of equality as working people was what determined whether she felt satisfied with her work or not. On the few previous occasions when she had worked for 'ladies of leisure', she had felt resentful because her employers could themselves have been doing what they paid her to do. She felt demeaned by that inequality.

This example really highlights the issue of satisfaction.

Why satisfaction matters

Satisfaction (or its absence) is what determines whether something feels like a chore or not. Satisfaction means more than simply feeling good inside when you've done something. It means that doing or having done something results in a feeling that you have *positively enriched your life*. However useful or beneficial something is, it can still feel like a chore, if it doesn't have this big, smiley-face result.

We take many beneficial things in life for granted. Teeth that don't need fixing because you regularly clean and floss them, electricity that comes on when you flick the switch because you paid the bill. Clothes that are clean and comfortable because someone washed and ironed them. Each of these could be satisfying in the positive sense I'm talking about – or achieving them could feel like a chore.

Things like good teeth, electricity at your fingertips and clean clothes make life easier and more pleasant because *they make other things possible,* and, of course, when they go wrong, we notice what we *can't* do or *can't* enjoy as a result. Most people don't experience them as being satisfying *in themselves.* Neatly weeded gardens, smooth-running cars and filing systems that let you put your hand on the document you need immediately you need it play similar parts in most people's lives. We'd rather not have to put in the effort to do the background chore that gives us the result we want because doing it is rarely exciting, enjoyable or satisfying in itself, but we know we really should make ourselves ... This chapter aims to help you find a way to change that – and so discover a new kind of enthusiasm for the chores in your life.

Choredom

I've heard it said that boredom is a state of wishing you were somewhere else. Chores are often experienced as boring, so, for short, let's call this combination a state of 'choredom'. Repetitive actions like ironing, jogging, weeding, washing up, doing repetitions at the gym, mowing the lawn, can all bring about choredom – but not always, and not for everyone. The very same actions can also be experienced as soothing, trance-like, consciousness-expanding, endorphin-producing ... Low-level recurrent activities like office documentation can have the same effect: for some people they don't feel a 'real' part of the job they wanted and signed up for, yet for others they can be a satisfaction in themselves and a benchmark of competence and achievement.

Choredom is created by the way we think.

What makes the difference is the way you frame the activity – because framing makes all the difference to the way you feel. The activity is in itself neutral: it becomes 'boring', 'tedious', 'soothing', 'dull, 'challenging' or 'satisfying' to *you* because of *your* previous experience and your attitudes.

Changing a frame that isn't helpful

A state of choredom often has its roots in the past, but you don't have to be ruled by past experience. Being nagged as a child to tidy your bedroom, put away your toys, do your homework and so on can soon teach you to nag yourself when you face the adult versions of such tasks. One option is simply to recognise this and remind yourself that that was then and this is now. However, changing long-established attitudes and reactions that have become automatic isn't simple. The old mantra 'mind over matter' implies a struggle with yourself in which you try to subdue your natural or immediate reaction by denying what you feel and telling yourself how you ought to feel instead.

Become a curious and intent enquirer.

A more effective strategy is to pay real attention to the moment-by-moment detail of what your choredom actually involves. Are you making your lawn-mower lines really straight (or intriguingly curved)? How many steps do you take to a single breath when you're jogging? What's your system for washing up? Everyone has a system, even if it's just starting with the top item of the pile in the sink and working their way down. How strange it is that you choose to do it like that, rather than in some other way. When I was young, someone taught me a routine for ironing shirts – first cuffs, then sleeves, then the shoulder panel, then one front, followed by the back and other front and finally the collar. I find this little miracle of method very satisfying. I wonder who my shirt-ironing mentor was, how old I was when they taught me and why I have always done it in that same exact way ever since.

It is this specialised mindset – one of curiosity, with its intense yet relaxed focus – that can set off the mind's alpha-wave patterning, producing the spaced-out feelings and endorphins and the sense of wellbeing that comes with them. It is as if consciousness was temporarily focused down into a single point. Could you bring yourself to approach cleaning your car in that way? Or getting receipts together and prepared for your expenses claim?

What's your reason for getting started?

We can all think of something we really need to do, and perhaps even want to do, without feeling motivated to do it. Are you someone with hundreds – perhaps thousands – of photos stored in your computer, who can't find that image you wanted to show someone, or to polish up in Photoshop to get it even better, because your filing system is so unsystematic? Are you sure the insurers never sent you that letter they said they did – but even if they had, you wouldn't know where you'd put it? Want to draft a proposal at work, but can't seem to find that crucial article you remembered reading a couple of months back? Pinpointing your reason for doing something – the benefit it delivers to *you* – is a useful beginning.

Motivation means having a reason for movement, and one way to generate this if your mammoth involves chores is to create what NLP calls a *compelling future* which will transform how you feel about it and make it seem positively inviting.

Creating a compelling future

Just imagine feeling differently about your choredom mammoth. As you wonder – perhaps doubtfully – about the possibility, you are already beginning to engage in a miracle of the mind. Your mind. The miracle is that when we imagine something in advance, the very act of imagining starts to set off the reactions we would feel if that same something were happening now and for real. If we imagine something exciting, our heart rate goes up. If we imagine something frightening or difficult, we start to feel anxious. If we imagine something soothing and pleasant, we breathe more deeply and slowly. Right now. Just by thinking. The future that we've been creating in our imagination is already compelling. Like the majority of our mental processing, its ingredients are the familiar ones of sight, sound, taste, smell, feeling and touch. The brighter, crisper, clearer, louder, more active and more tactile these components are, the more compelling the future they create. And the reverse is also true. A fuzzy, pale, small and static image of tidying up, cleaning the car or getting your desk clear doesn't really stand a chance!

Using your mind to draw upon the stored experience of your senses is something you've been familiar with from childhood, even if you were not aware of how it occurred. Once you do know about it though, you can make it happen deliberately; and you can use it purposefully to help you create your own choredom rescue package.

TRY THIS:

1. Imagine that you have *already* completed your choredom task. How do you feel?
2. Now reflect on exactly what's going through your mind. Which of your senses are most involved? How motivating (i.e. strong, interesting, vivid, energising) is the information you are giving yourself?
3. If you don't feel pleased, excited or satisfied at having done your task, pick one sensory element – for example, the pictures you were seeing in your mind's eye – and hype it up. Recreate it bigger, brighter, larger. Does that make a difference? Keep playing with the different kinds of sensory information till you get a change – fortunately, this kind of experimentation only takes moments.
4. Now go back a step. Think through the actual process of doing your choredom task, noticing the same kinds of things. Do you need to amplify, brighten or intensify the way you imagine the doing?

Years ago, I used to help my mother with her quilt-making. Her role was to select fabrics and colours and do the handwork. My job was to do what felt like the dull, heavy and uncreative work of machine-stitching the patchwork blocks together, adding a padded lining and a fabric frame and, finally, backing the finished article with a huge sheet. BORING. What got me through it was the vivid image I kept before my inward eye throughout: the finished quilt hanging over the wooden balustrade in Liberty's London store, visible to shoppers on three floors and all sides. On occasion, several of my mother's quilts would be on display at once, and they were sold to buyers all round the world. That was the compelling (mainly visual) future that kept me doing my part as I sat at her kitchen table with my sewing machine or crawled around her floor with a handful of pins.

Getting yourself on side

Creating a compelling future for your choredom task sets the scene right. But there are still many ways you can actually get it done. Finding the way that works for you is a matching task that relates to your personal stamina, energy and bite-size preferences (see Chapter 3). It also helps to take into account another aspect of your approach to life: whether you are most comfortable doing things in an orderly manner or experimentally. In NLP, these two contrasting ways of going about things are referred to as *procedural* and *inventive*.

Getting beyond choredom can actually be fun.

Here's a menu of tactics that have all worked well for me and for people I know, including clients, friends and colleagues. As you read through the list, notice how you respond to the different strategies, just as you would mentally test out the items on a list of appetisers in a restaurant. Try out the ones that activate your taste buds! As in a real restaurant, you may be drawn to the more tried-and-trusted favourites or to the playful, experimental or downright wacky ones. It is fine to stay with what feels natural – you need to co-operate willingly. Equally, you may find that if you go beyond your comfort zone and try out a strategy that feels quite strange – even alien – to your usual style, it could actually deliver what you want. It's entirely up to you.

Plan a small reward for afterwards – cup of coffee, phone call to a friend, fifteen minutes with a book or magazine.

Try at least one item from this taster menu today:

1. Repeat bookings

If your task crops up regularly (for example, washing up, cleaning, filing, accounts, doing assignments), you might enjoy assigning the task to a designated time in the day or the week or month.

A self-employed bookkeeper that I knew travelled a lot to see his clients. He created a daily routine for keeping his paperwork in order and up to date. Before he got out of his car when he arrived home, he scooped up all the receipts for his day's expenses and other paperwork relating to the visits he'd made. Once inside the house, he made a hot drink (small reward) and took it to his desk to sip while he entered everything directly on to an expenses spreadsheet he'd created on his computer.

Then he filed any papers that needed filing, and made a short list of things that would need following up. Only once he'd 'put work to bed' like this did he feel happy to let his working day end and his personal life restart.

One mum I knew got her housework done by assigning each day its regular chore: by the end of the week it was all done. Her children knew that Monday was sheet-change and washing day, on Tuesday the kitchen chairs would be upside down on the table when they got home from school and the floor would have been washed and the rest of the house vacuumed, on Wednesday clean ironing would be stacked in the airing cupboard and on beds ready to be put away, on Thursday Mum went shopping and on Friday the shelves of the walk-in larder would be filled with cakes, bread and pies ready for the weekend.

2. Pinball wizard

This one works well for people who like to surprise themselves into random acts of virtue. You can use it for any kind of tidying activity at home or at work. Set yourself a time limit if you want to (or make use of an odd half hour or so) and stop as arbitrarily as you started.

Start by picking up something – anything – that needs shifting or putting away. Deal with it, and once you have put it away or filed it, pick up the nearest something else that needs processing. If you are hanging up the washing, what's the nearest thing in the bathroom (or the garden) that needs to be dealt with? Take it where it needs to be and look for a third something. You are going to ricochet from one object to another, one place to another, getting a whole series of small satisfactions as you put stuff away, plus some amusement and physical exercise en route.

You can tackle desk tidying and filing in a similar way. Don't attempt to be methodical: start with the uppermost piece of paper on your desk and find it a proper home. If you haven't already got a file for it, create a new one. Don't attempt to sort stuff out within existing files – that's another job for another day. If needed, create a file called 'Stuff' or 'Throw away?' What you want to start with is the look and feeling of order. You are not trying to fool yourself that you have created a complete workable system out of chaos – only that you have made a start and retrieved some surface space as a bonus.

3. Random strike

This one's for those smaller, non-recurrent domestic tasks you somehow never seem to get round to doing. For example, reorganising the contents of your kitchen cupboards, sorting out a pile of stuff to take to a charity shop, deciding which items currently sitting in the garage or the shed could be taken to the tip, sifting through the things in your airing cupboard. In itself, an instruction to be random rather than systematic can be really liberating – it feels naughty, but still gets the job done: a win–win combination! This way of beating choredom works well with children for exactly the same reason.

If you are a linear thinker and list-maker, these items may

keep appearing on your to-do lists. Forget the lists! Instead, write each task down on a separate piece of paper. (Leo and I find that the back of previously used and now unwanted A4 paper torn into quarters affords the right amount of space for this.) Put all your task papers in a large bowl and shake to shuffle. You may even want to designate a special bowl and throw your 'to-do' ideas into it from time to time as they occur to you. Making the to-do a random matter like this adds a touch of spice to doing it. Whenever you have a bit of time, or feel the urge, take the first piece of paper that comes to your hand and do whatever's written on it. When finished, tear the piece of paper ceremoniously into small, small bits and celebrate. You could even create a matching collection of small rewards in another bowl to give yourself a practical pat on the back when you're done.

4. Saved by the bell

This one is good for lengthy or unavoidable stretches of choredom at home or at your desk. It is also good for getting children into doing their chores. You will need a timer – watch, phone or kitchen variety, depending where you are – and a reward occupation that can be sandwiched with your task. (A reward occupation at work might be spending time on a task or project you actually enjoy.) Set the timer for twenty minutes and blast at your chore till the timer goes. Sigh with relief, set the timer again and wallow in your reward occupation until the timer goes again. Do not cheat – either way! Even if you are making good progress with the chore, force yourself to have your reward space! If you are in the middle of a fascinating sentence in that novel – drop it! Enjoy the randomness. You can do this on–off sand-wiching for short or long periods of time, depending on stamina (yours or other people's) or how close you're get-ting to finishing (just one more burst and it will be done).

5. Turning chores into projects

For some people, the very thought of repetition is choredom in itself. Yet many tasks do repeat. This strategy relies on changing your estimate of a task's importance, and really shows up the usefulness of being able to think flexibly about breaking things down and building things up. It's not the inherent size of the task that matters, but how big it seems to you. Bite-sizing is all!

Often, we try to make the job seem smaller by telling our-selves 'It will only take half an hour' or, 'If I do a bit every day it will soon get done.' This is a breaking-down strategy, and it can work well at some times, for some tasks and for some people. However, trying to minimise a task in this way doesn't always help. It can sometimes be more effective to chunk up the way you think of it instead, so that you feel it's worth doing and it seems more of an accomplishment to complete it. One way to do this is to designate a repetitive task as a *Project*.

- Let's start with emails. How many are sitting in your in-box right now? There are 251 in mine, of which 27 are unread, and 421 are in my sent box – and I'm aware that for many people at work these numbers will seem neg-ligible! Do we really need to keep all these? And, if so, do we need to keep them in unsorted heaps? (Just as I wrote this, and quite coincidentally, my computer offered to compact them to save me disk space!)

Time to create a system that works! The possibilities are as endless as your inventiveness (and that is far greater than you may think). Systems are very personal things and, in my experience, most of the ones suggested by experts can be as daunting to use as not doing anything at all. I hope, however, that you'll take the following suggestions as just that – suggestions.

What you're looking for is a way to chip away at all those little electronic 'envelopes' and corral them into appropriate homes. To do that, you first need to delete all the ones that you don't need or want. Start with yesterday's emails on the basis that today's haven't reached urgent status yet.

1. Open each one in turn, even if you opened it yesterday, and if it's junk *delete it at once*.
2. If it contains useful information, reread it and decide if you need to file it – in which case, create an appropriate file in your cabinet or computer and file it there at once.
3. If it needs referring on, refer it on. Pass over the ones that need answering until you have got rid of the rest.
4. Now you should just be left with a group that need active thought and decisions. Have you time to deal with them now?
5. If you have, get started. Create files for these as you go – the aim is to get them out of your in-box and into their own designated spaces.

6. If your time now is limited, earmark a space later today or, failing that, tomorrow. Answer all the need-answering ones as soon as you can.

7. If you have time to spare after that, go back to the day before yesterday's intake and use the same method to deal with that.

8. If you have another twenty minutes or so (see Chapter 13), go back to the *very first* emails in your in-box. How many of these are still worthy of storage? Be ruthless. Paperless office does not mean multi-mega-bites of hard drive clogged with ancient stuff. As a test of whether an item needs keeping, ask yourself if it is worth printing out and filing. If it is, do that. If not, bin it! You don't have to be your company's (or your family's) archivist.

- Ironing is another chore you can approach as a Project. Instead of feeling guilty about it, you could deliberately leave it all until you're beginning to run out of some essential items, designate that Sunday afternoon for The Ironing Project, set the board up in front of the television and iron till you're done. (One of my own recent Ironing Projects involved twenty-two shirts, two pairs of trousers, five table napkins and ten handkerchiefs and took one and a half hours. I found it very satisfying!)

- If you still wear shoes that need cleaning, you could gather every shoe in the house into one room, enlist helpers from the family if you want and can, and set up a production line. You could separate out the processes and work on one at a time till all the shoes are done; you could allocate each helper, if you have them, their own task and work the shoes along the line till the last person administers the final polish; or you could deal with every single shoe as a separate entity. Half the fun is that it's up to you.

- If housework is going to be your Project, try taking a single room at a time and really go to town on it. During that week give that one room all your housework time. Leave all the rest. With a week's worth of housework time, you should be able to make a real difference – and you won't have to look at it again until every other room has had its turn.

6. Bring in the troops

For big, lengthy or onerous jobs, get help. Pick on friends or family members who can be relied on and who won't be judgmental about your reluctance to manage on your own. Offer bribes, swaps or other rewards. Build in some fun if you can: help me paint the house at the weekend and I'll provide the barbecue; help me go through my wardrobe and I'll help you with yours; help me do that car-boot sale and I'll – what would you like in exchange? Even, clean my car and I'll clean yours; come supermarket shopping with me and we'll have coffee together afterwards.

People sometimes talk about going through fear and coming out the other side. I'd like you to leave this chapter with the exciting possibility that on the other side of

Cutting Mammoths Down to Size

choredom you can find a place of ease, stimulus, fulfilment and even joy. Also, of course, one of feeling as proud of your own ingenuity in adapting your approach and changing your thinking as of actually getting those chores done.

6

Complex Mammoths

Some mammoths are pretty straightforward, but others seem just too complex for you to know where to begin. You might be trying to compare options that aren't comparable; you might have to make an immediate decision about something now, even though not all the information you need is yet available; or perhaps you feel unable to take any decision at all because each mini-decision you think about seems to lead you round into another that seems to need making first ... and that one into yet another one ... so it feels like you're in a labyrinth.

Big tasks and complex problems can occur anywhere. They can involve work and home, practicalities or tangled webs of feeling. However, there are some simple steps you can take to unravel it all.

Problems can be easier to solve if you have a problem-solving system.

TRY THIS:

Here's a step-by-step strategy that will help you disentangle a complex mammoth, so you know what it involves and where you can make a start on managing it. I'm going to illustrate it through the stories of two of my clients, taking you through their experiences step by step.

Step 1: describe your problem

When we tell the story of our mammoth, to ourselves or to a friend or professional helper, it helps us move away from the detail that's currently occupying us, so that we can start to clarify underlying issues or questions that need to be addressed.

Jenny had worked in the training department of a large private company for fifteen years. She liked her work and her colleagues, and had twice been promoted. Then the firm was bought out by a rival, and as part of the new organisation's 'rationalisation' a large number of people in both the original companies were made redundant or had to reapply for their jobs. Everyone felt very anxious.

Jenny thought she had better start looking at job adverts, just in case. One job really attracted her, but it was based about an hour's drive away. She applied anyway, for the experience, though she wasn't sure that she really wanted the job, and was surprised to be asked for an interview. Her partner said she should accept the interview appointment because the job paid better, even though it would mean a lengthy commute. So Jenny said yes; but almost immediately her manager made her a different offer, which really stumped her.

Jenny's manager explained that to save the ongoing costs of permanent staff, the training department was going to be closed and training bought in, as and when required. She offered Jenny a vacant post in the personnel department instead, and tried to persuade her to take it, even though much of the work would be unfamiliar. Jenny was told she had to make up her mind overnight, and her boss implied that she should be grateful for the offer. That was when Jenny phoned me.

The more Jenny thought, the harder she found it to decide. Should she take the personnel post, just because it offered continued employment, and if she didn't take it there'd be others who would? When I asked her: 'Whose problem is this?' Jenny began to realise that though she had to make the decision, she was not responsible for creating the problem itself. That came from the company's need to reorganise. In a strange way, she felt better once she understood that some of the urgency and uncertainty she was feeling was being transferred on to her by her manager. Conscientious people often assume responsibility when they needn't.

My other client, Paula, had been in a bad marriage for years, but put up with her husband Alan's abusiveness for the sake of the children. We had worked together for some time, and she'd eventually decided to leave him.

Cutting Mammoths Down to Size

Almost within days of her making this decision, Alan had a bad car crash while returning from his firm's Christmas party. One leg was badly shattered and would almost certainly have to be amputated. It was also near Christmas. So for both these reasons Paula postponed telling him of her decision.

Step 2: work out what you really want

Ask yourself what you really want. Getting your end goal clear is important in itself, and asking you to frame a longer-term goal takes you away from your current confusion and gives you a guideline towards a future you want and can start to shape.

What Jenny wanted was a meaningful job that fitted and used her expertise and that offered her some autonomy.

Paula still wanted to leave Alan – but she knew she'd feel very guilty if she did, and she believed the kids and Alan's family would think this was a wicked thing to do.

Try to get your end goal really simple and crisp in your own mind, like those in the above examples. Aim for a short phrase that sums it up.

▶

Step 3: recognise the obstacles you're dealing with

When you try to articulate your end goal you may, like Paula, get distracted from the simple core of what you really want and find yourself arguing internally about how difficult, impossible or unpleasant the path to achieving it may be. You may be saying things to yourself like, 'But that couldn't happen because . . .' or, 'But then that would result in . . .' or, 'But in order for that to happen X would have to do Y and I can't make them do that.' Pay attention to these internal arguments – they are usually important clues to what's getting you stuck and keeping you there. Objections to change can refer to the past (it's always been that way), the present (I'm stuck with this now) or to the future (if I did that, then X would be bound to happen), so you can see at once that they are a very important part of what's keeping you stuck with your mammoth as you already know it. You might find it helpful to write these internal objections down.

Once you get these assumed obstacles out in the open, you can more easily understand the contribution your own thinking is making to the size of your mammoth, and you can begin to challenge yourself. You can ask yourself questions like: 'Is it really the case that that couldn't happen, or that this would inevitably result?' 'How do I know that I couldn't do anything about that?' 'Could I find a way to show that person that this would actually help them as well as me?'

The root of these internal arguments is usually an

▶

assumption you're making about 'how things are'. We have to simplify in order to make sense of the world, but though it's essential, simplifying has inherent drawbacks.

NLP identifies three types of simplification: we can *distort* information, *delete* it and *generalise* from it. Distortion usually involves interpreting what's happening in the light of what you expect, fear or are used to. Deletion means overlooking something – either because you just 'don't want to see it' or because you are overwhelmed and not seeing straight. Generalisation means taking one event or observation and thinking and behaving as if it were always, or never, the case – interpreting an event in the light of that 'rule of thumb', rather than examining it carefully in its own right.

Bringing your assumptions to the surface by putting them into words allows you to start examining how they may be affected by one or other of these processes.

Step 4: make it clear to yourself and others what your mammoth actually involves

Focus in. Tease out. Pinpoint. Jot your findings down in detail. Plot the connections between the components too. The thigh bone really is connected to the hip bone! If your problem feels circular, you might want to put your items in a circle. If you feel you are zigzagging from one thing to another like a ball in a pinball machine, try drawing in the zigzags. Where things lead on to and out of each other, put

▶

arrows. Use colours, if it helps. Make the issues visible and alive in a way you couldn't if you were just putting them in a list.

Specifying just what your mammoth consists of helps you disentangle its complexity as far as decision-making and possible actions go.

I asked Jenny to list the practical advantages and disadvantages of each option. Were any decisive in themselves? She jotted down the following answers:

Personnel job. *Advantages:* Same firm, same pay, no change to domestic arrangements. *Disadvantages:* Less autonomy; new things to learn – not sure if working in a different field would be enjoyable; would need to obtain further qualifications in the new field, in order to take career further.

External job. *Advantages:* Chance to use existing skills; stimulus of new environment; positive move, rather than 'making do'. *Disadvantages*: Might not be offered the job anyway; travel time and expenses would increase; less free time outside work.

Then I asked Jenny to imagine she was looking down on the situation from a great height, able to see every detail in relation to the problem as a whole. When she did this she realised two important things: first, that her anxiety about having to decide about the in-house job before knowing about the external one was blinding her to the bigger opportunity of reviewing her skills and her career as a whole; and, second, that it had made her forget that if the training department was being closed down, she would probably be eligible for redundancy.

Paula's situation raised strong and conflicting emotions. Whatever she decided to do would impact a number of people who were important to her and make a difference to how she would be judged by everyone she and Alan knew. For herself, she wanted out. She wanted freedom from Alan's bullying, but she knew that Alan's family and friends saw him not as she did, but as a jovial 'rough diamond' of a man, and they'd ostracise or even attack her. But there was more: if she deserted a disabled husband like this, would a divorce judge think her fit to have custody of the children? Could she even live with herself? Those were her fears, but Paula realised that that was all they were – fears. What she was overlooking was the need to get professional legal advice and help.

Taking a gods' eye view like this can help you realise that you actually have more information or clearer priorities than you thought you had. Feelings often block the flow of information from the back of your mind to the forefront where you can use it to create a richer picture and discover more possible interventions. Data that is held unconsciously, or simply overlooked, can sometimes make all the difference once you prise it out of its hiding place. Be curious. When talking with any other people involved, be as open and as clear with them as you can.

▶

Step 5: what are the simplest things you could do?

Highlight what items are most accessible, and others that are urgent and 'won't keep'. You are looking for simple ways to get something moving, and these are two routes to begin with. Remind yourself that small and simple changes can sometimes have disproportionately large results, because any change has knock-on effects. It may be enough to send one email, make one phone call, do one thing differently (or not at all) in a repeating pattern to make that first shift.

Jenny now knew she needed more information. Without this, any decisions would not be fully informed. She pinpointed the following possibilities, and decided to act on them right away:

1. To ask for an immediate interview with HR about redundancy eligibility and concerns.
2. To inform her manager that she couldn't make a firm decision until she had this information.
3. To seek external legal advice, if necessary.

As soon as she got into work the next morning, Jenny phoned the HR department and made an appointment. Then she went to see her manager, taking a friend and close colleague along with her to act as a supportive witness. The friend made notes of what was said, in case of possible misunderstandings, and also went with her to the HR appointment. By the end of that interview, it was clear that Jenny would be eligible for redundancy, and she informed her manager in writing that on this understanding she was not willing to take up the internal post. However, she did decide to keep the external interview appointment as she still wanted a meaningful job, despite the redundancy.

Paula got out the local Yellow Pages and made some phone calls. She called a number of lawyers who said they specialised in divorce. She asked around and, eventually, found the number of a women's refuge in a nearby town – 'just in case'. While the kids were at school and Alan was still in hospital, she searched local papers, noticeboards and the job centre for posts that provided living accommodation. She knew she needed to do her homework before she leaped.

Step 6: what's the worst outcome you can think of?

Ask yourself: 'If I took the wrong approach, what would be the worst that could happen?' Scary as this sounds, when you really think about it there are few decisions in life that are entirely wrong – and precious little chance that you could be sure in advance which they were going to be, anyway. Sometimes, 'Just get on with it' really is the best advice to give yourself. Taking action changes the stuck scenario: things will be different afterwards. Managing the new scenario you've created gives you the chance to start

▶

again, to be in charge and to shape what happens in future – you've made an impact on your mammoth and, in so doing, you've proved to yourself that you no longer need to be its victim.

Even though Jenny was clearer in her own mind about the personnel post, her future was still uncertain. The worst outcome would be that she'd have to live on her redundancy money, or even sign on for a while once it ran out. As her partner was working, they could manage for a while if they had to. 'We've talked it through, and we're both sure that it would be bad for us both if I was committed to a job that wasn't right – so there's really no other decision to take,' she said.

The interview for the external job went well and Jenny felt appreciated, but another candidate did even better, so she wasn't appointed. Two months after the interview, she was offered another, and even more appropriate, job elsewhere.

Paula could imagine only too clearly the worst that might happen. Even a disabled Alan could get drunk and violent, if he felt provoked – but she had suffered that and survived it before. She thought that a living-in job might give her more protection than living on her own somewhere. She knew Alan's family would be hostile – she could face them if she had to. She dreaded the kids turning against her, but hoped that once away from the constant tensions and rows they would begin to accept the idea. Thinking this through hardened Paula's resolve, and she went off to see a divorce lawyer.

Step 7: have you missed anything?

You may have gone through the steps so far, but can you be sure that you've really thought of everything? Well, here's a way to find out. Every situation in life involves at least one of the NLP Neurological Levels, so you can use them as a checklist. (For a more detailed explanation of what they involve, refer back to p. 54.) Ask yourself what your complex mammoth may involve on each of the levels.

1. Practical considerations and constraints (Environmental factors)
2. Actions taken, not taken or needing to be taken (Behavioural factors)
3. Information and skills (issues of Capability)
4. Assumptions and principles (Beliefs and Values, both yours and other people's)
5. Issues about yourself as a unique individual (Identity)
6. Issues about personal meaning in the world (Life-purpose). Not every personal conundrum involves something as significant and charged as your ultimate life-purpose, but it's always worth checking out whether it might reach that far and that high.

▶

All of these are important where mammoths are concerned, but the ones at the end of the list are often crucial – and, just as often, unrecognised or hidden.

Let's run an everyday example through the list. The television you bought turns out to be faulty (Environment); it's obvious that it needs to be replaced or the money refunded (Behaviour). To be sure of your position when confronting the retailer, you will need to find the purchase receipt and, perhaps, read up the retailer's policy and conditions for returns (Capability – what you know and the skill with which you handle the other person). These steps are relatively straightforward. However, it's more than likely that in this case your real mammoth actually stems from your Beliefs and Values. For example, you might be thinking something like: 'I know I'm in the right, but confronting the shop will probably involve hassle and unpleasantness, and I'm never good at thinking straight when someone makes me feel I'm being a nuisance, or when they try to convince me I'm not entitled to something.' Buried in here is a belief about how effective you're likely to be in confrontation. Or you might be thinking: 'Actually, I think I'd prefer a straight refund, but what if they offer me a replacement instead? That would mean me having to stand my ground twice, not once.' In thinking like this, you're assuming that seeking a refund is going to be difficult because the shop assistant will offer you something you don't want.

Cutting Mammoths Down to Size

I remember once envisioning exactly this kind of scenario when I wanted to exchange a garment I'd bought for my daughter that turned out to be too small. Apologetically explaining this to the assistant at the returns counter, I was astonished when she said: 'No need to apologise. If you weren't here with a complaint I wouldn't have a job.' End of story! And a very useful learning experience for me.

An apparently minor mammoth like this one is unlikely to impinge on your Life-purpose, but it could certainly involve important issues about who you think you are and how you'd like others to think of you (Identity). Are you a peaceable type? How would you feel if someone thought you were 'difficult' or 'a troublemaker' or 'someone who stood on their rights'? If you feel uncomfortable about any of these, your apparently straightforward mammoth of returning faulty goods involves deep and important issues about your identity and place in the world. No wonder you keep putting off making the trip to the shop – perhaps even to the point when the time limit for returns runs out.

Once you've identified the real ground your mammoth is standing on, it becomes much easier to disentangle the issues, de-invest the emotion and get on with the job. In the process, you may also have begun to demolish a slightly different and more significant mammoth than the one you thought you were dealing with. In doing what was needed to make it smaller, you've also been making yourself bigger and stronger.

Mammoths are not absolute but relative.

7

The Burden of Obligation

The mammoths I was exploring in the previous chapter faced my clients with urgent decisions prompted by complex practical considerations and in-built time pressures. In this chapter, I want to unpick the challenges posed by mammoths involving more diffuse emotional issues such as obligations and burdens. I'm going to do this by examining some common, yet controversial, sources of obligation and resentment such as Christmas, debt, gratitude and loyalty to family.

What freight is your sense of obligation carrying?

Every mammoth has the potential to arouse powerful feelings, but the burden of obligation often experienced in relation to these issues is among the most likely to 'push your buttons' and to concern you at the higher logical levels – your beliefs, your values and your sense of who you are.

Though it's possible to feel hemmed in by a sense of obligation at work, you're more likely to feel like this in your important domestic relationships such as friendships and family life, so that's where this chapter focuses. One reason is that each of us has been a child and feels at heart indebted to our parents. This feeling is often deep and unconscious, and owes as much to the relative helplessness of children and the perceived powerfulness of their adult carers as it does to any realistic assessment of whether the upbringing itself has been 'good' or beneficial. Growing-up physically doesn't automatically mean growing-up emotionally, and when we're with members of other generations old patterns of feeling and responding frequently get triggered even when they're no longer appropriate. Family loyalties are as strong as they are sometimes puzzling, and help keep us tied in.

What turns an obligation into a burden?

One important factor is guilt. Guilt often accompanies a sense of obligation: the feeling that we are in some way substandard is readily evoked in most of us when we try to do what is wanted, needed or expected by others. Guilt does more than make us feel uncomfortable or inadequate: it often has a paralysing effect and makes it hard to know what we really want and to act on it. In other words, guilt can make us less authentic, whatever age we are.

A second factor is a feeling of discomfort about being indebted. Human beings seem to have an in-built sense of exchange and 'fairness' and, as various studies have shown, this results in people going to considerable lengths to repay what they perceive as a debt. We feel more comfortable if our exchanges with others more or less balance out. This seems to apply equally to debts that are small and specific – for example, a loan of goods or cash – as to ones that are as complex and unquantifiable as the exchanges of chores and favours within a family. When you feel someone else 'owes you', you are likely to feel irritable or even angry. But you will probably feel just as uncomfortable when the debt goes the other way – people don't like to feel under an obligation, so when you can't repay a debt, you feel trapped and compromised. The actual debt in such cases is usually far less of a problem than the *feeling of indebtedness.*

A number of things could be involved.

- You may feel that you have no prospect of discharging your debt, and perhaps no way of knowing what you could do to discharge it anyway. For example, how can any of us 'repay' our parents?
- This sense of powerlessness may lead to you resenting the person or situation you're indebted to. Then you can go on to feel guilty about your resentment . . .
- You might believe that because you have in some way benefited from the other person (for example, they have done you a kindness) you have no right to gripe or object.
- Your very sense of who you are, who you want to be or even could be could start to feel compromised. It's possible to feel inadequate, dependent, resentful, even belittled, through being the recipient of someone else's generosity.

A third factor is the likely 'cost' of changing things. Dealing with an established obligation will inevitably have knock-on effects, and runs the risk of rocking the boat. One way or another, there's a cost involved in making changes, and often this is what stops us making them. The important thing, though, is to bring that cost to the surface of your awareness – and perhaps to other people's attention too. Once you know what you're paying and in return for what, you can decide if it's truly worth it.

Feeling comfortable with being indebted

What makes the difference between feeling comfortable with being obliged to someone and feeling trapped? It could be knowing what you have to do to discharge the debt (pay back a loan, have friends you recently visited to stay with you next time). It could be understanding, perhaps for the first time, that the other party made the indebting offer freely – perhaps even cheerfully.

Some years ago, when we were very hard up, some good friends quite unexpectedly wrote us a cheque for a thousand pounds. 'We can spare it, and we don't want it back,' they said. Sometime after this, when we were in a better financial position, we learned that another friend of ours needed some money urgently. We asked for his bank details and transferred the sum he needed into his account. We were aware at the time that we felt good about 'passing on' the generosity. I think now that a kind of repayment was involved in our minds. We knew we didn't need to repay the loan itself – there was no obligation between us and our friends other than one of affection. Rather, what the experience set off in us was a free-spirited, joyous, generous impulse based on similar feelings of warmth, friendship and – above all – equality.

Finding a way to freedom

In my experience, what matters most is that you feel you have a *choice*. People can accept all kinds of obligations and make all kinds of compromises, without feeling compromised – provided they believe they are free to choose. Two similar stories with contrasting consequences illustrate this clearly.

Les was a client of mine many years ago who suffered from migraines. He had explored various forms of treatment, and was on medication from his doctor. In fact, it was the doctor who sent him to me because he thought other issues were involved. When Les first got married, his wife had made it clear that her widowed mother was going to live with them, and Les had not felt able to object. So for years, there had been 'three people in the marriage'. Les got on reasonably well with his mother-in-law, but he did resent the fact that he had to share his wife's time and attention with her.

As time passed, the mother's health and temper deteriorated and Les's wife Ruth became an involuntary carer. This meant that the couple's social life was curtailed because one or other of them always had to stay in the house and, eventually, Les's wife also had to give up her job, which she had greatly enjoyed. By the time Les came to see me, his home life more or less revolved round an irritable and infirm old lady and the migraines Les had had intermittently for years were now both regular and severe.

One day, I asked Les how he was feeling about the home situation. 'Oh,' he said, 'I get by: I just put her mother to the back of my mind.' As he spoke, he became aware of his hand lifting to point at the exact place where he reported feeling most pain from his migraines. 'So that's what I do with her,' he said wryly. 'She's the pain in my head.' This was the beginning of a careful, thoughtful process of sorting out – in his own mind first of all, and then in discussion with his wife – how they could manage in future. The key fact they'd been missing was that the obligation they had taken on at the beginning of their marriage had changed significantly. A healthy middle-aged woman with her own independent social life had now become infirm physically and mentally and, as a result, a full-time, long-term dependant. Making this explicit enabled Les and his wife to see that they needed to take the big step of finding her mother a place in a care home where she would receive proper nursing support, allowing them to re-establish the 'normal' married life that had been eroded away almost without their noticing. And, perhaps not surprisingly, the gaps between Les's migraines started to get longer and their severity diminished.

Ron is a friend we've known for many years. He was a teacher who greatly enjoyed working with his adult students and built an interesting career for himself. When he was in his late forties, it became clear that his mother, who lived hundreds of miles away, was developing dementia. His elderly father was finding it difficult to cope and, after long and careful thought, Ron decided to let his house and care for his mother for as long as necessary. He relocated and moved in with his parents, becoming his mother's companion and carer while the illness gradually worsened and both parents became even more frail. On one of the brief visits Ron made to check on his house and his tenants, I asked him, rather tentatively, how he was finding all this. I was surprised and impressed to discover that he felt no sense of resentment at the major changes that had taken place in his life. He was fascinated by the fluctuations in his mother's ability to understand and relate to her situation and to her family, and he said that one of the biggest things he had discovered was that within the context of the daily support and presence he was able to give, his mother could communicate far more effectively than anyone had thought possible. Ron set himself to explore the latest research that was being done on dementia and its treatment, and remained with his parents until his mother eventually died. Only after his father also died did he return to his own home and work again.

These two contrasting examples illustrate how very different the sense of obligation can feel, and how much it depends on the beliefs, values and attitudes you are able to take into the situation. It's not a moral question – whether you are 'good' or 'bad' about accepting what happens to you – but rather a question of how you frame the obligation within yourself and how easily it 'sits' with who you feel you truly are.

What can you do if you feel you don't have a choice?

As the Star Trek character Mr Spock once said, 'There are always alternatives.' But often we are unable to see what that they might be. The step-by-step disentangling strategy I outlined earlier (see pp. 92–104) can be just the tool you need to help you realise you do have choices after all, and to pinpoint just what they are. Let's look at something that can cause more than its fair share of misunderstandings: the question of how to manage Christmas.

Is Christmas all it's supposed to be?

Over the twenty years I worked as a therapist, one of the commonest problem topics my clients brought up was Christmas. In my office, the annual what-to-do-about-it countdown usually started in early autumn, and the corresponding what-went-wrong-and-how-can-we-prevent-it-happening-again unpicking often went on until Easter. The widely shared and widely hoped-for ideal is that Christmas is a 'family time' in which relations come together to enjoy each other's company with the luxury of relaxing, enjoying good food and drink, meeting friends and generally celebrating. If you are lucky, this may be your experience, but the reality is often very different: people can feel pressured to spend money they may not have on gifts, food and home decorations, and most spend hours shopping, cooking and passing time together without the usual distractions of everyday life, and with little means of escape from what irritates them about each other. There's a whole raft of obligations here! If your last Christmas was like that, you may well feel anxious, angry or trapped as this one gets closer

At the same time, you are likely to feel guilty because 'Christmas should be a time to look forward to and enjoy' and because you know that deep down you really love your relations. (If you are ambivalent about any of them, that only adds to your discomfort.) You are caught in the trap of obligation: a belief you should do something you may not want to do, either in the way that's expected or not at all, and a further belief that even feeling like this about it is somehow wrong.

So you can feel guilty about something like Christmas whether you are a parent or grandparent hosting the event or a teenager or young adult wishing you could be doing your own thing elsewhere.

Managing this web of buried assumptions and feelings can be taxing, but the same disentangling pattern used in the previous chapter gives you a structure to tease apart the components and find new ways forward. I'm going to take the example of my clients Jen and Harry to show you how this can help.

Step 1: describing the problem

Describing to yourself or someone you trust just how you experience your 'problem Christmas' can bring assumptions and feelings that have been buried to the surface. In identifying just how the reality you are dealing with fails to match up to the common ideal of this festival, you can begin to discover just what it is you really want to change. Hopefully, you will also begin to accept that the difficulties you may have experienced or be anticipating are not necessarily your fault – or, indeed, that of the others. In-built in the current Christmas ideal are some issues that can cause most people stress at any time:

- Money
- Being confined with the same people for any length of time
- Spending time with people you might otherwise not choose to spend time with
- Change of food, drink and sleep patterns
- Lack of the focus and activities you're used to in daily home and work life.

Identifying which of these may affect you, and to what extent, can in itself open up useful and quite manageable possibilities for change. Should you cook – or eat out? Do you have an 'open house' or should you set a time limit? Perhaps bearing in mind the old adage 'fish and guests stink after three days', my mother once asked us to tell her how many days she would be welcome for. It must have taken courage on her part, but it helped make the 'Christmas contract' both crisp and even!

Harry was the first person in his family to get a professional qualification. His parents owned and ran a market stall, so they were delighted when he qualified as an accountant, though at the same time rather disappointed that he didn't want to follow in their footsteps with the family business. Harry was very successful and took delight in being able to buy himself a large house, provide his parents with a new car and treat them lavishly when it came to presents and festivals such as birthdays and Christmas.

After a few years of hosting extended family parties over the festive season, Harry's wife Jen got resentful about the work and the cost. She felt they were being taken for granted and exploited by aunts, uncles and cousins because, in everyone else's eyes, they 'could afford it'. Harry felt he owed it to his parents to be generous, and he couldn't see a way to streamline things because, as they all saw it, 'family is family and families share what they have.' It was only when he and Jen started to bicker about this that they thought of getting some help.

Step 2: asking what is really wanted

I have often reminded clients that they can make any concession they are prepared to – but that concessions are only meaningful and acceptable if you *first get clear with yourself what it is you really want*. People sometimes think this is 'selfish'; but without establishing what you want, you have no firm base for making requests, dealing with requests from others or negotiating something acceptable in between.

By asking Jen and Harry what they really wanted, I got them to admit – to themselves as much as to me – that their own preference would be for a quiet Christmas with just their own children and parents.

Step 3: recognising the obstacles

Where mammoths involve others, changing them is going to involve some discussion or explanation. And often it's the fear of confrontation or conflict that stops you saying or doing anything.

As they went through these steps, Jen and Harry began to realise that a fear of explaining their feelings and wishes about Christmas to the rest of the family was a powerful block to making any change. They were frightened that however they did this, their families would still feel hurt and rejected.

Step 4: making it clear to yourself and others what your mammoth actually involves

Mammoth feelings like dissatisfaction, unhappiness or resentment aren't usually invisible, even if you don't actually mention them. People sense the presence of such emotions, even if they're not willing to talk about them. A strategy I've found helpful in cases like this is illustrated by the metaphor of 'putting your fish on the table'. This idea comes from the hostage negotiator George Kohlrieser (see Further Explorations, p. 222), who started helping fishermen with their catch one day while on holiday in Italy.

As they slapped each fish on the table to gut it, Kohlrieser realised that there was a very important metaphor in all this: fish guts are not wanted when you eat the fish, and the sooner you remove them the less trouble they cause. If you don't get the guts out, they fester and your fish is ruined.

The same is true of things that bug you about other people. When you don't tell someone they've upset or disappointed you, that unexpressed 'fish gut' can start to rot your relationship. If you 'put it on the table' for discussion while it's fresh it can be dealt with and disposed of quickly before serious damage is done, and the 'feast' offered by the good parts of the relationship won't be spoiled.

Often, though, you may be able to avoid the tricky area of personalities by focusing on practicalities instead, and that was the approach Jen and Harry decided on.

What could Jen and Harry do about their Christmas dilemma? Should they put up with the usual formula just because it had become a tradition? Should they tell the others the usual festivities were cancelled this year? Should they just invite the family members closest to them – and, if so, what excuse would they offer to the rest? None of these options seemed at all workable. They had to make a different kind of change – one that shifted and redefined the formula entirely.

Step 5: highlighting the simplest things you could do

After a lot of thought, the strategy Jen and Harry employed was to offer to host a family party for everyone else on New Year's Eve and to book a short Christmas break for themselves, their children and their parents in a hotel abroad. That way, they changed when and for how long they were going to welcome members of the extended family, without pulling out of welcoming them entirely.

'Much less work, much less cost, but we're still offering the others something they can enjoy, if they choose to come,' Jen said with satisfaction.

Step 6: learning from worst-case scenarios

As part of thinking their options through, I asked Jen and Harry what was the worst they thought might happen as a result of changing the Christmas 'tradition' they'd all got used to. And then I asked them to assess how they'd feel if these 'maybes' did actually happen. These are some of the things they came up with:

- Some members of the wider family might be hurt or angry. But these were people Jen and Harry felt obliged to see, rather than ones they really wanted to see, so actually they wouldn't mind all that much.
- Perhaps people – in the wider family and their friendship circles – would gossip and say they were being 'mean' to stop hosting the usual house-party

celebrations. If this happened, and they got to hear of it, of course Jen and Harry would feel hurt. But, they realised, no one can control what's said about them behind their backs; and if the price for keeping the entire family happy was to continue buying their good opinion with lavish treats, then the meaning of 'family' was not worth much, anyway.

Step 7: double-checking in case you missed anything

As a precaution, go over the issue and your thinking once more before you act, just in case ... Then go ahead and act.

In summary, unpack what your obligation really involves:

- Identify who or what makes you feel trapped.
- What is the 'running cost' of your debt (i.e. what does it make you do or stop you doing?)
- What would you have to do to discharge your debt?
- Would there be any negative consequences in making a 'final payment'?
- What do you want to change?
- Are you willing to rock the established boat by discussing how you and the other people in the situation feel? If you cannot change the situation, or are unwilling to accept what you expect to happen if you do, can you find a way to think of it differently and so change your internal experience of it?

In this chapter, I've explored a number of real-life examples of different ways in which people can frame and reduce a sense of obligation in order to manage it differently. In the next chapter, I'm going to look at issues and burdens that are buried in layers of past events and feelings. I call them 'historical mammoths'.

8

Historical Mammoths

The mammoths we've looked at so far have all been current. You are either struggling with them now or anticipating struggling with them in the future. But what about mammoths created by events in the past? What about old wrongs and injustices that still make you smart? What about mistakes you once made, opportunities you lost or times when you weren't proud of yourself or gave in to others and regretted it? These can be mammoths too; and though they may seem buried in the past, they can still be consuming your energy and thought. Can you do anything about them?

Of course you can. Regrets, grievances and unfulfilled wishes that have remained powerful in your awareness can all be managed in new and more effective ways. People often describe things like this as 'unfinished business': it's been said, wryly and I think truly, that when something is 'unfinished business', what you really mean is that things didn't turn out how you wanted them to. In this chapter, I'm going to explain how you can reclaim the energy you're investing in this kind of mammoth, so that you are at last able to let go and move on. I use the present tense – investing – because every time you think about it, every time you mind how it turned out, every time you wish things were different you are adding to your original investment of emotion and energy.

> **Mammoths that are not dealt with are like black holes in your personal universe: they still have the power to suck you in.**

What does 'letting go' involve?

When people tell you to 'let go' the implication is that it's quite simple. There's an 'ought' hidden in the very idea – it's almost as if it's not only possible, but morally superior to tell yourself to forget and move on. Just how easy is that, really?

Years ago, the teenage son of some close friends of ours was knocked down by an elderly driver driving too fast. Our friends' son was just sixteen, on his way home midevening from an event at school, when a car came zooming along and clipped him as he crossed the road. He died soon after. Though the police began a prosecution for dangerous driving, this was hardly a consolation to his parents.

It's not possible to forget something like this, it's not easy to forgive – and it may not be appropriate, either. But for as long as you go on raging, your mammoth is still taking charge of you, however much time has passed since it first came into your life.

Real letting go involves being able to transform or withdraw the energy that's directing your thinking, feeling and current behaviour from the past situation or event. Our friends decided that they would take their son's birthday as a yearly opportunity to celebrate his life, instead of mourning his brutal death.

Letting go means undertaking a number of things:

- First and foremost, you need to stop hoping that things will change. Mostly, this is a wish that somehow other people will at last come round to your way of thinking. Get real. You can't make them. The only person you have the power to change is *you*. All the time you have spent wishing they would come round to your way of thinking has been time spent stuck in a victim role.

- You need to give up the victim role, whether it's expressed through the way you relate to others or the way you have been thinking about yourself. It can be cosy being a victim. You don't actually have to *do* anything. As soon as you accept that this passive place of suffering is where you've been, you can ask yourself if you want to stay there. If not, step into the new, challenging, perhaps even difficult (and sometimes exciting) role of someone who makes things happen. Whatever initiatives you take will change the situation and get it rolling again. Even if you don't get everything right, you won't be stuck any longer.

- Accept that even if you made a mistake or mistreated someone else, you had your reasons at the time. People don't deliberately set out to make mistakes – they do what seems best at the time. If you now think you were selfish or unjust, you'll need to face how it makes you feel about yourself. You will also have to get your head round the idea that one bad action doesn't make a bad person. If you've made the same mistake more than once and think there's a pattern at work, accept it and explore with yourself how you can change it. If someone wronged you, honestly ask yourself whether this was intentional or accidental – or simply the wrong thing done for what seemed to them at the time the right reason?

- Be realistic about what's possible here and now. You cannot rewind to the time when ... What could you do now to unshackle the past mammoth and allow it, yourself and perhaps also the other person, to move on again?

- Work out strategies to achieve a better situation and a better sense of yourself in future. Maybe you can apologise for your wrongdoing. Even if the other person has died, it's not too late to express your anger or regret: write it down, put it somewhere safe or have a ceremonial burning and clearing of the air. The important thing is to clear the mammoth debris out of your head.

- Maybe it's time for a 'fish-on-the-table' session (see pp. 117–18) with whoever else was involved. Remember that you cannot *make* them learn or see things differently. Maybe you will just have to recognise that they have moved on, and that it's your relationship with you that needs mending. Allow the energy you have freed up to be reinvested again. Reinvestment might take the form of new projects, new ways of behaving or setting out to acquire new skills. Or it might simply mean that once you have come out from the ancient mammoth's shadow, your world has altered: you notice things differently, appreciate them more and experience a sense of lightness, freedom and excitement that's been missing for a long time.

The history of your mammoth

You need to remind yourself how your mammoth first got created. Tell yourself the story, noticing how much consists of facts and how much of interpretations and judgments. It may help to write it down – it will make it easier to spot the judgmental words as you reread it. The way you have told your story to yourself all this time isn't just an account – it has become part of the mammoth itself. For example, here's one of mine.

In my twenties, I worked at Sussex University as an administrator. I started doing some part-time teaching, and then took the risk of resigning my permanent job to take a one-year lecturing post, filling in for a colleague on leave. The year after and the year after that, other colleagues went on leave and I substituted for them. Then a permanent lecturing post became vacant and I was encouraged to apply for it. Feeling confident that the job was mine, I regarded the interview as a formality, barely prepared for it and was relaxed and informal with the interviewers – all colleagues whom I knew well. I was astonished and outraged when they chose someone else. As I worked through the time that remained before my year's contract finished, I felt convinced that I had been hard done by, and even in later years when I happened to visit the campus, I resented the unknown stranger who was doing 'my job'. I even felt sometimes that I had been let down and betrayed by people I liked and trusted. I felt victimised.

Revisiting this story reminds me how much I'd done to set myself up for that role. It never occurred to me that all posts had to be advertised, and that a job at a prestigious new university would attract applicants of high calibre. Being the insider didn't automatically make me the most suitable person. I never thought I'd need to put in a special effort or make out a case for myself, and never dreamed that my friendly colleagues would put quality before comradeship. All these realisations came much later, after I had spent a good long time feeling pushed out, unwanted and undervalued. How much easier it was to blame them rather than myself. I felt wronged – but the rock-bottom fact was that on the day there was a better candidate.

Rewriting the script

Once you pay close attention to the way you've been telling your story, you can start rewriting it. You can't change the facts, so these need to be highlighted and accepted. What you can change is the meaning you make of them and the way you let them script your attitudes and behaviour in the present and future.

The metaphor of scripts helps us realise that where other people are involved there are two possible ways of changing the impact of the past. Old scripts can be revised to improve things in future. Sometimes you may be lucky enough to get the other person's co-operation in this rewriting. This happened to a client of mine called Jodie.

Jodie took her dog, Mitzi, to obedience classes with a local trainer, Jason who, in turn, offered to take Mitzi to a show or two to give her the idea and show Jodie how best to manage her. So far, so good. Mitzi quickly learned how to behave and even started winning. For a while, Jodie enjoyed being the proud owner, watching from the ringside; but then she started to feel that Mitzi was becoming Jason's dog, not hers.

Eventually, Jodie felt that the only way out of the situation was to give Mitzi to Jason. She decided to get a new puppy and vowed she would never let anyone apart from herself have anything to do with it.

But since she wanted to train and show her new dog, she couldn't avoid meeting Jason or hearing about him. When she and Jason met, she wasn't herself. Sometimes she tried to charm and flatter him. That felt like a pretence. Other times she was resentful and distant, and that wasn't the real her, either. The mammoth of what might have been was there all the time, festering, at the core of her interests and her social life.

With the help of our sessions, Jodie realised that in the story she told herself, Jason had taken advantage of her inexperience, made her feel inadequate and ended up taking over her dog. What she was only just beginning to understand now was that she had been equally responsible for letting this happen.

Jodie decided to write to Jason explaining why she was so strange whenever she saw him, and to make it clear that she now felt that neither of them had been to blame. She told him she believed that they had both acted as they thought best, without foreseeing possible consequences. She hoped he'd be willing to meet her, so they could put the past to rest and find a way to be more at ease with each other in future. And that was what happened.

Jason too was sad about the way things had turned out. At the end of their meeting, they gave each other a hug and parted with good wishes and a smile. Jodie didn't feel they'd meet up again, except casually; but she did feel that the mammoth was dwindling away at last – perhaps for both of them.

What if your 'fellow actors' are not so co-operative? Even if this is the case, you can make real and lasting differences if you change your own 'part' by changing the way you see the situation. This will inevitably change your words and actions too, and so the cues you give your fellow actors will spark different responses in them – creating a different and, hopefully, better script for the future. Eddie's story illustrates how this can start to happen.

When I worked as a therapist, Eddie came to see me because he really didn't get on with his parents. His elder brother had died at fifteen in a car accident. Eddie was gay, socially unconfident and had always felt he was being compared unfavourably with his confident, outgoing, straight brother, rather than accepted for himself. After the accident, he felt his parents idolised his brother and undervalued him even more. Eddie did his best to be an acceptable son, but the older he got and the more nothing changed, the more upsetting he found the relationship. In fact, he was thinking of cutting his parents out of his life entirely.

What Eddie didn't realise was that every time he thought about them, or told himself or his partner an episode of his story, he was continuing to feed this ancient mammoth and keep it alive. Every time he followed the familiar script and tried to please his parents, he was reinforcing his sense of alienation. Every time he wished they'd change and see him for who he was, he was digging himself a bit further into his helpless, wronged victim role. Someone once described this as 'the triumph of hope over experience' – and giving up hope that his parents would change was actually the first, very bleak and painful, step towards Eddie's liberation. He decided to tell them how he really felt, and to offer them the choice of accepting him, flaws and all. He couldn't prevent them idolising his dead brother, but he felt he had a right to expect them to treat him better. In particular, he wanted them to accept his partner and make them welcome as a couple.

In recognising how he'd contributed to his own victimisation, and setting some requirements for his parents' behaviour in future, Eddie was starting to free himself from the mammoth to which he'd been linked for so long and to reclaim his right to define the current situation.

Seeing the mammoth with new eyes

Not all mammoths are as accessible as these. What can you do if you have lost an opportunity for ever, or suffered a huge knock to your sense of self, or if too much time has gone by for anyone else to really care about rewriting the story?

It's at times like these when you have only yourself to rely on – and that can actually be all you need.

One client of mine, Rachel, realised late in life how angry she still felt with her (long dead) father for having made her give up a boyfriend when she was in her teens. It was her first important relationship, and she had often wondered how different her life might have been if the relationship had continued. It wasn't that she hadn't had a really good life – just that other options had been taken away from her. She'd been clinging on all these years to a mammoth of possibility, and with it a sense of loss and anger towards her otherwise much-loved father.

*

Another client, Barry, had enjoyed his job managing a small and quirky department within a larger company – until it was merged with another department that had been more traditionally run. Barry was asked to manage the new super-department, and this turned out to be a disaster. Before the merger, he'd been personally liked and professionally valued: he knew he hadn't changed in his new role, but the way people responded to him and judged him did. His old staff felt dispossessed and neglected; and the ones from the other department resented his casual and informal style and thought him a poor manager with no leadership ability.

After several months of worsening atmosphere and declining performance the Board abruptly decided to restructure in a way that would make Barry redundant. He felt the whole process had been badly and insensitively handled from the beginning, and though he was relieved to be away from the daily pressures and tensions of work, he felt both raw and puzzled. He knew that his friends felt he'd been wronged; but being made redundant made it impossible for him to learn how most of the people he'd managed felt or why things turned out as they did.

Time went by for both my clients, and their lives improved. But these isolated and daunting mammoths in their past remained as powerful and upsetting as ever.

So long as you keep on telling the story of the past in the way you always did, the 'reality' it represents remains

the same. Only when you change the emphasis of the story, do you give yourself the chance of discovering a new 'reality' – that is, another set of meanings – in it.

Fortunately, they were both willing to take another look at the situation and themselves. They had quite a lot in common:

- Something they valued had been taken away from them without their consent.
- As a result, both felt they had lost a future they could have enjoyed.
- Even more importantly, their sense of self had taken a massive knock.

Rachel thought of herself as a loving person – but ditching her boyfriend hadn't been a loving thing to do. What helped was allowing herself to accept that her beloved father had indeed done one bad, even unforgivable thing – because he loved her and wanted the best for her. And she also knew that however sad she'd felt, her life hadn't been permanently blighted or warped.

Barry couldn't be sure whether he was or wasn't a good manager, but he was able to realise that it was the change in circumstances, not anything in himself, that made the difference. His style had suited his old department and his old staff perfectly, and brought out the best in them. But he began to accept that the very same qualities were quite unsuited to the new staff and the needs of a larger, newly merged, department. None of what happened was actually anyone's fault, though with hindsight he saw that everyone – himself included – had been insensitive in the way they handled the crisis.

TRY THIS:

1. Tell yourself the story of your mammoth. Keep a sharp eye – or ear – out for assumptions, judgments and signs of having taken up a victim role.

2. Imagine yourself into the shoes of the other person, or people, involved. How might they have felt and thought? What can you learn from taking their perspective?

3. Retell the existing story – perhaps even writing it down – including only events and facts and leaving out emotions, assumptions and judgments. What can you learn about others, yourself and the legacy of the events by taking this third-party, 'observer view'? How can these learnings enrich you in the future?

4. This story has been an undigested mammoth in your personal history – a story that got too big, too emphatic and too emotionally charged. That's why it took up so much time, space and energy. In the light of all you've now learned, and using your bare-bones factual account as the skeleton, how would you now like to retell it, so that in the future it can assume its proper place as just one of the many things that

▶

you've experienced, learned from and been in some way enriched by? Tinker with it until you find a way to honour the past without being enslaved by it. Write your new version down to help ingrain it in your mind.

Peeling away the old stories that helped make sense of your historical mammoth at the time when feelings were raw can be like dusting or chipping away debris from an ancient artefact. What you discover is the structure underneath, bare facts that you can examine from different angles and evaluate in a new way.

Up to now, we've been considering ways to disempower mammoths by chunking them down into more manageable portions. Now it's time to reverse the process and explore how, bit by bit, you can chunk up to achieve your mammoth goals and dreams.

Building Up to Mammoth Achievements

9

Can a Leopard Change Its Spots?

Creating a new habit can seem daunting, perhaps not even worth attempting, yet if you build up to it in small chunks you can start building a whole new habit pattern naturally and immediately.

Why do people think that leopards can't change their spots? Answer: because spots are an in-built part of what makes them leopards. But leopards lack an essential element that humans possess – the capacity to self-observe. Once you can look at yourself and reflect on what you observe, you can change a great deal – if you want to, if you need to and if you are prepared to.

Think for a moment about the things that people normally recognise and remember about you, and that both you and they would assume were your fixed 'leopard's spots'. Let's see just how unchangeable they really are.

- Your physical characteristics. Many of these can in fact be disguised or surgically altered.
- Your characteristic individual way of moving. With

practice, you can change this quite significantly. People who take a course in Nordic walking, for example, learn ways of taking longer strides while expending less energy, and once the new pattern has become ingrained 'in the muscle', many people find that they continue to walk in this more fluid, upright and effective way, even without the poles. Once the Nordic habit has become automatic, acquaintances or even old friends might well fail to recognise them from their walking patterns alone.

- The way you approach tasks and problems. This may in part be in-built, but education, family culture and self-awareness can also shape it to a considerable extent. Different approaches and new skills may initially be grafted on, but if used regularly they can become not just an item in your personal repertoire, but a genuine part of who you are.

- Your attitudes and beliefs. Though these often form a kind of personal bedrock, they too can be modified through education and experience.

In other words, what you are used to thinking of as 'me' is rather more adaptable than you might expect. And the way any of us thinks about who we are is crucial in allowing us to change or in keeping us static.

> **Leopards are literally hidebound. We don't have to be.**

None the less, habit is powerful, so I'm going to start by exploring how you can destabilise it, so as to make creating a new habit in its place simpler and easier.

A good start is to clarify to yourself what you have been thinking about your habit-related mammoth up till now.

- 'I'm usually scared to tell people what I think of them, whether it's colleagues at work, assistants in shops or even my wife and kids, because I'm afraid they'll get upset or angry.'
- 'I hate the fact that my desk is always untidy.'
- 'I can never seem to quit smoking – it's my only real treat.'

In each of these examples the speaker is confusing what they do (behaviour) and how they feel (emotion) with who they are (identity). They are linking together things that are perfectly possible to change with something everyone is understandably reluctant to tinker with. When you use phrases like *always, usually* or *never,* you reinforce this kind of mental straitjacket you've got yourself in.

Write down what you think about your habit-related mammoth. Have a careful, honest look at the way you are currently describing it to yourself. How could you change your wording so as to help free your identity from involvement with the issue? What kind of statement would you like to make instead?

If your mammoth involves habit change, the first thing you need to do is to separate your sense of self from your patterns of behaviour. Like stalactites and stalagmites, habits are built up through hundreds, even thousands, of repetitions. As water flows and drips, it has the power to create and change landscape. In this chapter, the landscape we're exploring is you. And the power you're going to make use of to change that personal landscape is the power of new habits.

You don't even have to try to abstain from, or break down, your existing habit. You just have to create a new one that works better. And more effective soon outperforms less effective. So you need to find a straightforward, uncluttered, grammatically positive way of describing what you want. Your brain will find it much easier to process a positively framed idea, because there's no mental cancelling out to do. Let's return to those examples:

- 'I'm usually scared to tell people what I think of them, whether it's colleagues at work, assistants in shops or even my wife and kids, because I'm afraid they'll get upset or angry.' How about rewording this as: *'I want to be able to give people feedback clearly and confidently.'*
- 'I hate the fact that my desk is always untidy' might become *'I'd like to have an orderly desk.'*
- 'I can never seem to quit smoking – it's my only real treat' could translate into *'I'd like to find ways of rewarding myself that are compatible with good health.'*

Try out the differences between these pairs of statements for yourself. In order to think about the first version, your brain has first to call up the idea of the unwanted habit and then try to cancel it out. What don't you want to feel – *scared*. Now try the second version. What do you want to be? *Clear and confident*. The positive phrasing helps the thinker clear the debris of old experience and old feelings out of the way and give themselves a cleaner start.

TRY THIS:

Think of a habit you want to change.

1. Quickly write it down, using the first words that come into your head. For example, 'I'm bad at managing my money.'
2. Insert the word 'sometimes' or 'often' into the way you describe the behaviour you want to change – e.g. 'I'm often bad at managing my money.' Say it to yourself a few times. What difference does that make to how you feel and think about yourself in relation to this particular habit? We are all inclined to generalise on the basis of patterns, but the danger of generalising is that it makes us feel that something that often or regularly occurs is *always* going to occur: in other words, generalising can create a false sense of *inevitability*. Adding in little words like 'sometimes', 'often' or 'mostly' makes you aware that though there's a pattern here, it doesn't happen *absolutely every* time. And that, in turn, makes it easier for you to change.
3. If you were using ideas like 'bad at', 'stop doing X' or 'give up Y', redescribe the habit change you are seeking in positive terms. For example, 'I want to manage my money, so I live on what I earn.'

What fuel is going to drive your habit change?

Any change needs motivation. Some changes are negatively fuelled ('I might get laid off, if I keep on doing that') and some are positively fuelled ('If I can demonstrate that I'm able to do this task well, I might be given more exciting and rewarding projects').

Here are some questions that help you unearth what your fuel is going to be. There are blank spaces after each for you to jot down your answers.

Q: What is your real, personal reason for wanting to change? Be honest with yourself. This is where your fuel is going to come from.

A:

Q: Is your desired change fuelled by a carrot or a stick?

A:

Some people do respond more readily to sticks than carrots, but the trouble with a stick is that while it sends you forward, it doesn't help you select the right direction to go in! By and large, it's simpler if you can specify what you do want instead, in this case by translating negative motivation into its positive equivalent. 'I'd like to perform more consistently to my boss's standards' might be a useful first attempt – but you could probably improve it even further by thinking a bit more deeply about what you really want. Perhaps it's something like 'I'd like to be the kind of employee my employer really wants to keep'.

'Ought' and 'should' can seem to provide motivation, and often feel powerful; but they rarely provide the energy that's needed for real and lasting change because they tend to involve confusing emotions such as guilt, anxiety, rebellion and a sense of inadequacy. Put another way, you're less likely to own the wish to change if it comes from outside you – what someone else thinks or wants – rather than from inside.

Q: Is there an 'ought' or 'should' underlying your change project? Who or what is behind it?

A:

Starting to build your new habit

Your first step towards creating a new habit is to de-clutter how your current habit makes you think about yourself. For example, you might think, 'I do – or don't do – X'; 'I like – or dislike – Y'; 'I find Z easy – or difficult'. These are 'leopard's-spots' statements because they imply things like 'always' or 'because that's who I am': the very way you're thinking is becoming part of your mammoth.

I once had a client who arrived late for our first meeting – and again for our second. When she was late the third time, I asked her if she was often late for appointments. She laughed and replied: 'When I was little my mother used to tell me I was late for my birth and I'd be bound to be late for my own funeral.' Only then did she realise how this piece of thinking had shaped her behaviour – and why. Small children are very literal in their thinking, and who wouldn't want to be 'late' for their own funeral? Once she had taken this on board, she was able to put history to one side and think quite differently about being on time or being late. For her, it was rather like taking a picture (being late) out of its existing frame (being individual, not fitting into others' expectations) and putting it into another (being late is often seen as rude or inconsiderate, do I want to be seen that way? No I don't. I want to be seen as polite and professional).

Reframing like this is a concept often used in NLP, and it's a technique that can be both simple and powerful. My client *reframed* the meanings attached to her lateness habit, and by changing its meaning freed herself to alter her behaviour easily and immediately.

> **Your habits are not who you are. They are just what you've got used to doing.**

Think of people you know who already have the habit you want and use them as models

Even if you have never done something and didn't like the idea of doing it up till now, you might still be able to do it if you acquired enough fuel and access to the right information. Because you're sensitive on this subject, it's likely that you will have noticed people who behave very differently – that is, in your view, 'better' than you. It's surprising how much detail you may have unconsciously registered about how they go about being so different, as the following example shows.

A resourceful young woman I knew had always been very shy. However, because she was both efficient and reliable, she was asked by colleagues at work to contact a large number of people, some of whom she knew only slightly or not at all, in order to make arrangements for a departmental Christmas party. She had to organise dates, make restaurant bookings and approach everyone individually to get their menu choices and advance payments. Knowing how shy she was, I wanted to find out how she had managed. 'It was simple,' she said. 'I asked myself how an extrovert would have gone about it, and then I did that.'

The three Rs of habit change

Let's sum up where we've got to. In order to change you need:

- A **R**eason to change (your personal fuel) and
- A way to **R**eframe your current habit and feelings.
- This makes it easier for you to **R**eform your behaviour into a different pattern, perhaps by referring to information you already have about how other people do it differently (modelling them).

What does your desired habit pattern actually involve?

Begin by chunking down your desired habit into as many small bits as you can. You might find it helpful to make a mind or thought map.

- Put your central idea in the middle of your page, with a ring around it. This phrase should be short, and will probably be large-chunk and quite abstract. For example, 'Giving feedback confidently'.
- Around it, put all the specific behaviours you associate with it, giving each its own surrounding bubble too. Some examples might be 'speaking clearly', 'keeping eye contact', 'being specific', 'sticking to a few key points'.
- Draw lines that connect each specific behaviour to the central idea. It's likely you'll have other ideas that connect to some of them. Put a branch line out from the relevant bubble and jot each new idea down too. For example, you might know that people can take critical feedback more easily if you are first able to tell them they're doing OK overall. So your branch line might contain something like, 'headline good stuff first'. Another related branch line might be, 'best proportion for comments is 70 per cent positive to 30 per cent negative'. You are, of course, chunking down as you do this, and it's likely that these are going to be the easiest and natural places to start creating your new habit.
- When you have mapped out everything that occurs to you at this moment (you can add more later), use a highlighter to mark any that seem immediately do-able.

Simple Mind/Thought Map

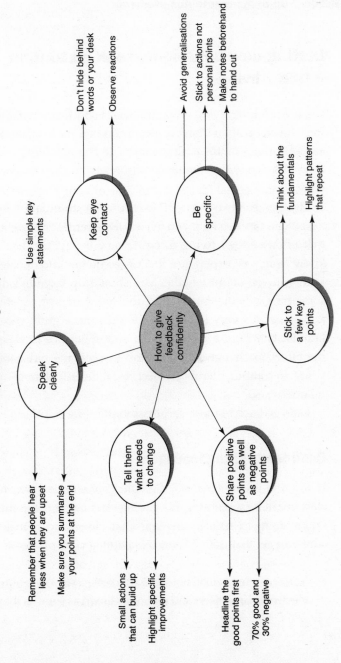

Letting new behaviour stack up to form a new habit

Once you've identified your simplest starters, you need to make them habitual from the very beginning. As I explained earlier (see p. 66), the easiest way to do this is to link your desired action with something you already do as a matter of habit.

Hijacking an existing habit to become the foundation for a new one can also help you bypass the internal arguments that often bedevil trying to create new behaviour. You'll know from past experience that once you get into debates with yourself about whether you should or shouldn't do something, whether you should do it today, or now, or later and so on, it's very likely that the mixture of guilt, sheer familiarity with the existing habit and reluctance to make the effort to change will combine to keep the old habit going. In computer terms, it's been your 'default pattern' up till now.

Let's go back to those earlier examples (see p. 141).

Confidently giving feedback

If you find giving feedback difficult, your simplest way to start might be something like getting clear about the points you're going to make by creating a list. How can you make sure you get that done? There are a number of options:

- You can carry a small notebook (or create a section in your electronic organiser) and jot points down as soon as they occur to you, rather than letting them swim around in your head, with the risk of getting forgotten or muddled.

- If the feedback is a formal requirement – as in staff appraisal – when you arrange the appraisal time, put another earlier time in your diary for you to do your preparation. It can be helpful to schedule this preparation 'appointment with yourself' for a different day, perhaps even a few days before you are due to meet your staff member. This time for reflection is just as important as your appointment with the other person. Once it's entered in your diary, the days will chug along and your preparation time will just arrive without any further effort. No cheating, mind – this is not an appointment you can change or skip!

Having an orderly desk

What's the first thing you do when you're about to sit down at your desk? Maybe it's hanging your coat up, equipping yourself with a cup of coffee or opening up your in-box. Tag your first, simplest orderliness-creating action to this. For example, *as soon as* you have done your chosen trigger action (hung your coat up, put your coffee down or clicked your mouse over your in-box icon) do *one* of the following:

- Remove five things from your desk that need throwing away.
- Or put any loose pens and pencils in the jar or tray where they belong. (Don't have one? Start a list with this as the first item to buy or bring from home. You're more likely to use a container you've chosen yourself.)

- Or take everything off the desk that isn't strictly relevant to today and put it in a pile on the floor or in a plastic bag. You will have to make time later for going through it, but you will have a clear desk and a clearer mind for today's work. You will also be starting to train your eye and mind to appreciate *space*.

You could, of course, do more than one of these – but don't be tempted! Picking just one action as a lead-in to your new tidiness pattern is the simplest and most effective way to combine the new action with one you already perform, so that together they create a new pattern that becomes automatic.

Finding healthy rewards

If you have been a smoker for some time, you'll have learned to overlook the fringe benefits of smoking, but these need taking care of too. Here are some that my clients have identified once they started looking more closely at the 'treats' smoking gave them.

- A reward I can give myself (not dependent on others)
- A break from choredom at work or home
- A chance to be sociable with colleagues
- A few minutes of personal 'down-time'.

You may recognise one or more of these. If you are to cut down, or cut out, your smoking you will need to find neutral or, better still, actively beneficial ways to replace whatever benefits it offers you.

One of my clients wanted to quit smoking. She was a waitress in a café before the law was changed to prohibit smoking in public places. When we looked for the benefits smoking gave her, she said at once, 'If I didn't stop for a fag every so often, I'd be on my feet all day – it's the only break my boss allows me. And it's a chance for me to chat to our regulars and feel like a person, not just a pair of hands.'

Fortunately, she got on well with her boss, and he agreed she could take some tea breaks instead of cigarette breaks in future. This made it easier for her to cut down and eventually give up.

Having identified some of the benefits, ask yourself what other small, free or cheap treats you could give yourself instead. Experiment with giving yourself one of these instead of a cigarette at some of your usual 'fag times'. Ring the changes, so you enjoy a sense of choice and plenty. You may be surprised at how quickly your old habit gets destabilised.

Here are some examples of other new habits my clients have created. You could take any of these that seem appropriate as a 'Try This' exercise.

TRY ONE OF THESE

- Taking a short walk from home every day after breakfast.

  This person worked at home, and the anchoring habit was breakfast. My client found that as well as getting

▶

fitter, she unconsciously started preparing her mind for the day's work – an additional benefit she had not foreseen. (You could take short walks from your office during your lunch break.)

- Planning the day first thing every day and briefly reviewing how it fits into the goals/targets for the week.

The anchor habit for this manager in an international bank was sitting down at his desk.

- Meditating every day for twenty minutes.

This stressed-out lawyer used to close his office door and lie flat under his desk. Initially, he set a kitchen timer, but soon found his target time became automatic. (There is more about the benefits of twenty-minute breaks in Chapter 13.) The anchor habit was an alarm set on his watch. He also trained his secretary to manage his diary to allow for the time-out breaks.

- Switching off from work at the end of the day.

This client didn't have to take actual work home to do in the evenings, but found that he couldn't switch his mind off. This made him tense and preoccupied when he got home, which caused friction between him and

▶

his wife and children. He used getting into his car in the office car park as his anchor: instead of driving off immediately, he took fifteen minutes to think over the day and 'close it down'. Sometimes he made notes, so that he didn't have to carry any 'baggage' overnight. Then he drove home with a clear mind and freer spirit.

We are what we repeatedly do, therefore excellence is not an act but a habit.

Aristotle

This chapter has focused on ways of creating a new habit. In the next one, I'm going to help you tackle a related but different issue: identifying the small chunks that will help you build up to a single major goal or achievement.

10

Bite-sizing Backwards – Your Personal Path to Achievement

It's time now to look at another kind of mammoth: the kind of major achievement you want to reach and enjoy in the future. It seems obvious that substantial projects and achievements won't happen overnight, but one of the things people mostly don't realise is that the way you think about them is what makes all the difference between success and disappointment. That's what this chapter is about.

'Begin at the beginning and go on until you come to the end: then stop,' was the advice given to Alice in Wonderland. It seems the natural approach. And when people imagine making their dreams come true, they usually expect to have to think forwards. After all, that's how time itself goes. This means they look for the best place to *start*. Actually, it's often better to do it the other way around. This was something Erskine Childers, who in 1903 wrote the famous thriller *The Riddle of the Sands*, expresses very clearly through his hero Carruthers as the story approaches its climax:

'We shall have to argue backwards,' I said. 'What is to be the final stage? Because that must govern the others.'

In this chapter, I'm going to introduce you to two powerful techniques. Over the years, I've found that if you put them together you can create a customised, precisely crafted route to achieve what you want. You'll be taking into account your unique situation and your individual needs; and because you know not only where you're aiming for, but also how you're going to get there, you'll be able to check at every step that you are on track, avoiding the kind of pitfalls that often keep people's dreams for ever out of their reach. This combination of techniques is what will give you the very best chance of bringing your own wished-for mammoth to vibrant, enjoyable life.

The first technique is an NLP one that shows you how to frame your goal so that it is actually achievable. The early NLP developers found that the goals people actually reached all had some key things in common. If you ensure that your goal matches up to these same conditions, it will, in NLP's phrase, be *well-formed* enough to succeed. You can use these criteria as a pre-flight check system, so you know what, if anything, you have to do or change before you set out. No wasted effort. No false starts. No dead ends.

The second technique was one discovered independently by two very skilful people. Milton Erickson, one of the outstanding therapists studied by the early developers of NLP, got his clients to imagine they had already achieved what they wanted – and then asked them how they got there. The brilliance of this apparently simple and natural question was that it instantly shifted the client's focus from the present, where they felt stuck, conflicted or uncertain, into the future, where the problem *had already been solved*. Once the client had mentally located themselves in the future, it was relatively easy to 'unpack' the details of how they had got there. Erickson's experience had taught him that people usually have a deep, unconscious understanding of their situations and what they need to do to change and improve them, but often can't access this information by thinking forwards. (Once this hidden information has been uncovered, other powerful techniques like making that future more 'compelling' in order to draw yourself towards it can also be employed.)

A similar approach was used by Barbara Sher, who wrote a book called *Wishcraft*. In it she also stresses that working mentally *backwards* from your goal is much more effective in helping you get there than working forwards. Years ago, a friend and I were thinking of writing a book together, and were advised by an NLP colleague: 'Don't start by thinking about what you want to write – think about who is going to want to read your book eighteen months from now, and then write it.' Sometimes the best way forwards is by starting at the end. I call the process Bite-sizing Backwards.

Goals help us make meaning out of our lives and give it purpose: they are the tangible representation of who we are, as well as what we want. Without them, we are left to the mercy of events and other people, ricocheting through life like pinballs, propelled by what the singer Paul Simon called 'incidents and accidents'.

I once worked with a group of young, able, ambitious men in an international corporation. At our first meeting,

I asked each one of them what he expected to be doing in ten years' time. Business was still booming then, and most of them expected to have made enough money to retire in their forties: holidays, sports and family time were what they mostly saw ahead. As we talked, I remembered one of my therapy clients who sold his successful company and retired at fifty. He was dismayed to find he had lost his sense of identity, meaning and purpose along with the business. I could see the possibility that some of these young men would find themselves with nothing lined up to engage all that drive, all that energy, all that creativity they now possessed. I could imagine that they too might feel puzzled, bored or perhaps even depressed.

Only one of these young men had a clear vision of a different, meaningful life beyond the corporation. He came from the East and was acutely conscious of the contrast between the lifestyle he and his family could enjoy in Britain and that of thousands of his contemporaries back home. So, unlike many of his colleagues, he saved and invested much of his salary, ran an everyday car, lived in a comfortable but not luxurious house and sent his kids to state not private schools. His dream for 'retirement' was to return home and help impoverished young people gain a better education and, with it, the possibility of a better life. In the jargon of business, it was clear to me that his dream was the one that 'had the legs' to become a reality.

Strategy 1: making sure your goal really is well-formed and achievable

To give your goal the best chance of succeeding, here's what you need to do:

- **Describe your goal in positive language.** We've looked at negative framing earlier in the book – and here it is again because it's very influential. It's not that negative framing is *wrong* – it's just that it *isn't enough*. Often, people don't go beyond wanting something to stop, or change. 'I want to stop being tentative in negotiations.' 'I want to stop saying "Yes" to my boss just because she is my boss, even when I disagree.' They don't know what they want *instead*. So they haven't begun to shift mentally.

  > **Thinking negative reinforces what you *don't* want. Thinking positive tells you where you're headed.**

  Asking yourself what it is that you *want instead* helps you formulate a goal you can actually work towards, and so begins the process of moving forward. For example, 'I want to feel confident when I'm negotiating'; 'I want to be able to say "No" to my boss when I think she's wrong.'

- **Be specific about what your goal means and involves.** How often have you heard someone say, 'I just want to be happy' or 'I'd like a decent lifestyle' or 'I want to be successful'? Words like 'happy', 'decent' and 'successful' are vague and in themselves unattainable. As soon as you ask, 'What is happiness?' or 'What is decent?' or 'What is success?' you'll see that to answer you have to supply much more information. And your answer is unlikely to be the same as mine, or his or hers because each of us starts from a different place and has their own definition of what the idea means *for them*.

I think of these generalised, abstract concepts as 'weasel words' – they sneak through our minds and our conversations and they are stealthy killers because we assume (rather than actually know) what they mean. That's why they are so often the source of confusion and misunderstanding between people.

If your goal is one of these nebulous concepts, ask yourself: What does happiness (or whatever it may be) mean to me? Delve deep until you hit a bedrock of real, clear meaning. What would a 'decent lifestyle' consist of? How will I know when I've got it? What evidence will tell me that I have (or haven't) got it?

- **Is the power to achieve your goal in your own hands?**
  Winning the lottery is not an achievable goal, because once you've bought the ticket, winning anything at all is just a matter of chance. Being left a legacy or spotted on the street as a potential model are the same. They are pipe dreams. The mammoth-sized dreams worth working with are ones you have a fair chance of actually making happen – because they are things you can

plan, learn, work for and arrange *yourself*. This is the time to be realistic and honest: what can *you* do?

Are you the one in control?

- **Build yourself a detailed idea of what your goal will be like when you reach it.** Where will you be? Who will be with you? What would you be doing on a daily basis? What will you be seeing, hearing, feeling, tasting, smelling? In other words, know where you're headed – through each of your senses. Is your goal an event (a trip around the world, a degree, a flat of your own) or a process (having more responsibility at work, writing a novel and getting it published)? By rounding it out in such detail, you give yourself some benchmarks for knowing how far you've succeeded. In addition, the rich detail you're building up in your mind acts in itself as a powerful magnet that will draw you towards making your own imagined future come alive.

- **Will you lose out in any way by getting it?** When you want something very much, the strength of your wanting can blind you to unintended consequences of achievement. All you see are the advantages of getting what you want, not the possible downsides: you are deleting a whole category of potentially vital information from your forward view.

  One man I worked with very much wanted a promotion – but the first thing he discovered when he got it was that the change in status affected his friendships at work. Mates weren't so matey any longer once he started managing them.

Many able people want to start their own business – but once you do you won't automatically be getting a salary every month and you may have to worry about finances or even go without pay at times. You wanted the freedom and autonomy – but did you want the anxieties?

Perhaps you wanted to escape from the rat race and live in the country – but did you realise how much time you'd be spending ferrying your kids around? Had you thought how long it might take to get from your rural retreat to visit friends and family – or the doctor, dentist or hospital?

Now's the time to construct a full and complex picture of what life could be like once your goal is achieved, and check out whether your dream really delivers what you hoped for.

Once you've gone through this checklist, reshaping your goal if you need to, you'll know that you've made it much more achievable – and worth achieving. Then it's time to use your imagination to create a bridge that brings you back to today – a bridge which you can then confidently use the other way about – to go *forwards*, step by step, to take you to your goal in reality.

Strategy 2: imagine having already achieved your mammoth – and then pin-point every single step that got you there

When the goal you're aiming for is a long way off, it can seem hard or even impossible to work out how you might get there. It can feel like trying to plan a voyage around the world or a trek across Siberia. You know it won't be enough to just put one foot in front of another – but actually it will, *if each step you take is the right one.*

The best place to start is at the end.

Working backwards is profoundly freeing. No ifs and buts to contend with – you're already experiencing what it's like to be there. Erickson had a phrase for this: he said that people 'know more than they know that they know'.

Barbara Sher says in her book *Wishcraft*:

Planning has to go *backwards* from the distant future to tomorrow ... but before you can put great deeds together in reality, you have to take them apart on paper to discover *what* small, steady actions, *in what order,* will really get you there.

Backtracking from something you're vividly experiencing in your mind allows you to realise exactly what must happen in order to make possible each stage of getting there – a sure-fire way you can then use in reverse order to build up to that dream mammoth bit by careful bit.

Bite-sizing backwards in action

Let's look at an example to see how this process can work:

As a youngster in his first job after school, Francis wanted to be able to do something for people who were less advantaged. He had grown up in New Zealand – now he wanted to be a volunteer in a developing country. Being realistic, he also wanted a fallback in case he became ill or ran out of money. So he needed some kind of profession. Teaching seemed an appropriate choice. What did he need to do first? In order to become a fully qualified teacher in New Zealand, he needed to spend two years training and to follow it up with a year's probationary teaching and two further years as an employed teacher in return for his state-sponsored training. All this was going to take him at least five years – but he knew what he had to do and what order it had to be done in.

If we plot out Francis' bite-sizing backwards steps, they look like this:

Volunteer in developing country

Become a teacher

Do two years' post-qualification teaching

Do one year's probation teaching

Do two-year training course

Apply for training course

Find out about teacher training today

How you can discover the steps that make up your bridge?

So how do you go about bite-sizing backwards from your own mammoth goal? It can be helpful to have a large sheet of paper – A3, if you have access to it, or you could use the plain side of shelf-lining paper or wallpaper. You need plenty of space, so as to help your thinking stay free and open, and also to allow room for any additional ideas and steps that may occur to you as you go along. I'm going to explain what you need to do, and then illustrate with an example of how mammoth goals might be plotted out into a series of do-able steps.

- Put your well-formed goal at the top right-hand corner of your paper. It's often a good idea to circle it with a balloon shape to make it stand out more clearly. This process is all about sharp, clear thinking and small, appropriate and manageable actions. Ballooning each item helps you make sure you keep each item tight, brief and distinct.
- Now ask yourself: 'What has to happen just before that in order to make it possible?' Put your answer in another balloon.
- What has to happen immediately before that?
- Keep asking this question and plotting down each answer in its own balloon, working downwards and to the left, until nothing else comes to mind. (If there are several answers to one question, plot them all down, side by side, and ask the 'What-has-to-happen-before-that?' question about each of them. You will now be

working with several parallel sequences rather than just one.)

- Now look at the item(s) that are at the bottom of your ladder of steps. They should be quite small and specific. Can you act on any of them today? If not, can you set a day and time in the near future? If not, has a step been overlooked or left out?
- Make a start on your first step today.

Let's take the example of one of my clients.

My client was an NHS clinical manager. He had been seconded for two years to establish a network of the different providers, groups and agencies involved in helping patients with a single serious physical problem, in order to improve the quality of the care each patient received and to get rid of overlaps and gaps in services. His role involved many emails, phone calls and face-to-face meetings to build and facilitate connections between allied professionals and voluntary groups. They all cared about patients in their own way, but according to their own agendas.

At our first meeting, my client described the challenge he faced. He said: 'The plan is a three-year plan. What I need to have done in eighteen months is have in place the mechanisms by which the plan can be achieved.' He would only be there to help for two years though, and he knew that the proof of his success would be that the system carried on effectively without him.

In order to help him think his way through this

limited time frame and plan where he could best put his efforts, I showed him how to bite-size backwards. Identifying what the NHS calls the 'patient pathway' – that is, the typical patient's journey through all the stages of illness and treatment and their encounters with the various support services – allowed him to see where the different agencies could connect and co-operate, and to consider where his own help and support would best support them.

He told me later that he had found the bite-sizing backwards technique so helpful himself that he planned teaching it to some of the leading professionals involved. That way, the skill would form part of his legacy to the project as a whole.

Life goes on after you've reached your mammoth

These two techniques are each powerful in themselves: as I've discovered in helping clients realise their ambitions at work and in life, once put together they can be truly trans-formational.

However thrilling it will be to have achieved your par-ticular goal, the world won't stop once you've got there. You won't have reached heaven, or a state of nirvana, or perfection – or even, necessarily, satisfaction. Your imme-diate goal, however important, is not the end of your personal life journey, but a part of it. It's worth considering, even now, the possible futures that await you beyond: what other choices, decisions and experiences will its achievement make possible? And whatever challenges and opportunities life may bring to you, bite-sizing backwards can help you manage them and even enjoy the process of doing so.

11

Reshaping Yourself

Have you ever thought that confidence was something other people had? Or wished you had the charisma to get served at a crowded bar, stand your ground under pressure or have others respect and look up to you as an authority on something you know about?

Where Chapter 9 looked at changing specific habits, this chapter unpicks the more pervasive kind of thinking that underpins your sense of identity and maybe holds a whole outdated self-image in place. Do you see yourself as others see you? Of course you do, because their impressions are being fed back to you all the time through a whole complex range of deliberate and unconscious feedback. However, because you too are sending out messages about yourself all the time, the opposite can sometimes be equally true.

Others see us as we see ourselves.

When you change how you see yourself, you will immediately start to modify the signals that inform others about who and how you are. Is it really possible to change something as habitual as your self-image? After all, you may have lived with your familiar version of you all your life. In my experience, you certainly can. It involves a bit of work, but not nearly as much as you might think. Let's discover how you go about it.

Attributes vs. commodities

The first thing you need to do is realise that there's a whole huge world of difference between '*I am*' something and '*I have, have not, or lack*' it. I call the first *attribute thinking* and the second *commodity thinking*. Let's look at what's involved.

Attributes are personal characteristics, part of the way people describe us. The word comes from the Latin noun *attributum*, meaning something allotted or assigned. The word 'attribute' is now used in a more personal sense to designate characteristics that people see as typical of us as individuals, such as 'clever', 'lazy', 'thoughtful', 'industrious' and so on. They are seen and felt as being part of who we are (our identity). To change any one of them implies changing something which is in-built. You can tell when someone's doing attribute thinking because they use words like 'am', 'is' or 'are' about the quality being described.

Commodities (from the Latin *commoditas*, meaning something fitting or useful) are possessions: things that can be acquired, bought, given and received. Perhaps you learned to speak tactfully – you *acquired* tact. People may still use the word 'is', as in 'he is tactful' or 'she isn't at all tactful', and this is where difficulties often arise. But when someone says that a person 'has tact' or 'has no tact', it's quite clear that they're talking about a commodity that the person being talked about has, hasn't or hasn't enough of.

TRY THIS:

Test for the difference by saying to yourself, 'I'm confident' or its opposite, 'I'm not confident'. Now try saying, 'I have confidence' and 'I lack confidence'.

Think carefully about how each of them made you feel. The chances are that you felt worse about the first pair than the second.

The difference is in how the words resonate within you, and that vibration can have profound effects. When you say, 'I am' or 'I am not X', it feels like you're describing something fixed, like the size of your feet or the colour of your eyes – you're identifying an *attribute* – something that's characteristic of you and, by implication, unchangeable. But when you say, 'I *lack* X', it's more like saying you've run out of sugar or some other finite thing – in other words, the abstract quality, confidence, has become a finite *commodity*. And finite commodities are things you can acquire, replace or stockpile. And when you do, the knock-on effects can be profound.

These differences in wording can be much more important than you'd think – because words have real power to shape not only what we think, but how we feel. And that's true whoever is doing the talking. When you think something in words, you're effectively saying something in your head. And when you say something in your head, *who do you think is listening?* NLP calls this 'internal dialogue': you're both the speaker and the listener – effectively having a conversation with yourself. When you repeat a thought or phrase to yourself over weeks and months and even years, you are likely to end up believing it's true, even when it doesn't have to be or perhaps never was in the first place.

Here's a personal example that illustrates how straitjacketing internal dialogue can be:

I have never thought of myself as *pretty*. I realised as I grew up that people found me *attractive* – but pretty, no. Actually, I went one stage further and thought of myself as *plain*. Nice eyes, cheerful smile, nose and chin that could kindly be described as 'perky'. Odd-looking combination. Get on with it, I thought, that's just how you are (spot the attribute thinking?). Then, talking to one of my students when I was already middle-aged, I referred in passing to being plain – it was a kind of throwaway, taken-for-granted, that's-how-it-is assumption made on the way to saying something else. But my student really heard me, and interrupted by saying, 'But you've never seen your face when it's animated'. Thanks to that single brief comment, I now have a much more complex self-image, one that I think is more accurate and *know* to be much more enabling: it's that of a face I can never see myself, but which I know isn't plain because it's almost always in movement. My student shifted me from 'I am' to 'I have' – in this case, it was something like 'I have my moments!' Commodity thinking, here I go!

Once you think of yourself in commodity terms, everything starts to free up, and change becomes easier to think of, to initiate and to manage. It's because you've stopped thinking about personal qualities as *in-built* and, instead, appreciate them as something *acquired*. You don't have to defend them as something that's integral to yourself, or try to remove them like a part of your physical body. Instead, you can work with them and modify them in much the same way as you might change your style of clothing or the furniture in your sitting room. You could think of this as a process of enriching your personal vocabulary. New situations, new words – and new possibilities.

Jeremy often struggled when he had to tell his staff what to do. He didn't think of himself as 'a natural leader'. Yet when he travelled abroad, and wherever in the world he was, people of all races and ages asked him the way when they were lost. The same man sometimes had difficulty getting attention in meetings, which confirmed his feeling that he wasn't charismatic. Yet in round-table discussions or complex negotiations, he was often the one who stimulated and supported ideas, brought people together and helped them find agreement. As we mulled over these apparent contradictions, Jeremy realised that he could lead, and, in the right circumstances, he did indeed have charisma!

Change can sometimes be instant

There's a common assumption that change is something that happens gradually, especially where relationships with others are involved. However, that's not always the case, as the following example shows.

I had a client in his late sixties. Roger seemed socially sophisticated and confident, but he had grown up in various households under the shadow of a number of mother figures, where he often felt bullied and inadequate. He still felt cowed by his one surviving stepmother. Now he was about to go and help her relocate to a new apartment, and he fully expected she'd make him feel like a small boy all over again ... He wanted to change this, and believed that with my help he could.

We talked about the dialogues between him and his stepmother: not just the words, but the tone and the body language. I pointed out that habitual patterns can often be derailed very quickly if one person 'forgets' or 'edits' their lines. Actors on the stage go into 'automatic' on a long run, but if something unexpected happens, such as another actor forgetting his part, they will be brought abruptly back into the real world and may lose track of where the on-stage dialogue has got to.

When I next saw Roger, he was overjoyed and astonished. The whole pattern of interaction with his stepmother had changed and he felt grown-up and equal. 'I can't remember what I said – it might even have been just my tone of voice that was different,' he told me. 'She was going on at me in the old way. Somehow, I responded differently – and everything changed between us. And, what's more, *stayed changed*.'

Had Roger changed who he was? No – but he had significantly changed the way he responded. He had interrupted the familiar 'script' they were both used to. It only took a few moments, but after that, both he and his stepmother knew the balance of power in their relationship could be different. And once you know something, you can't *un*know it. You can, of course, choose to ignore the new information – but that is still an important difference from how things were before. You used to feel you had no choice: now you know you do.

For Roger, one change was enough. In his case, the change had been intuitively made on the basis of the discussions we had been having; but this isn't the only way to change. You can engineer change more deliberately.

Wearing down and building up – the effects of repetition

Self-image is usually built up over time. It's been argued that the 'you' that you think you are comes from the expression you see as a baby in your carer's face. You internalise *their* sense of you as *your* sense of yourself. No doubt, there's an element of truth in this, and it seems to be supported by research on children's school attainments, which showed quite shockingly how often they came to fulfil the low expectations their teachers had of them – even when these teachers had been given incorrect information about their potential.

The families we belong to at home and at work (teams and departments count here) have their own way of shaping different 'family members' – not usually through conscious intent, but through the way they habitually describe and behave towards each other and, in so doing, reinforce (or fail to reinforce) different qualities: 'the ideas person'; 'the funny one'; 'the lively one'; 'the difficult one'; 'the good networker'; 'the hard-working one'; 'the pretty/good-looking one'; 'the slow-but-sure plodder'. You can probably think of examples of all of these in your own personal and professional families. Over time, these attributions often cease to register consciously, but they can have profound unconscious impact. Like water dripping on stone, they can build you up or wear you down. The qualities attributed to you may not reflect the 'you' that you'd like to be. Or you may want to make a change. Perhaps it would be fun to be 'adventurous', rather than 'reliable'? (Or, of course, the other way about.)

So far, I've been talking as though we are all equal, with only the quirks of our families and friends to reckon with. But of course, that's only part of it. All kinds of qualities can be attributed to people because of their social status, their race, their nationality, their gender and their sexual orientation. If you suffer now, or have done in the past, from prejudice, you're a victim of attribute thinking. Even with a positive attribute, as in the statement, 'I'm a natural multitasker because I'm a woman,' there is still the potential to lock you in, minimising your personal ownership of the quality by attributing it to your being part of a more general group. Recognising just how extensive and powerful attribute thinking can be when it's applied to whole groups, and to individuals because they are part of one of those groups, helps us manage its impact on ourselves and others more sensitively and skilfully.

I'm not saying that we should endeavour to get rid of 'I am' statements and 'I am' ideas – only that we need to be very vigilant about how they're used and the limiting effects they can have. (We also need, of course, to monitor how we may be affecting others by the way we describe them.) It's a whole lot easier to change a commodity than an attribute: think of changing what you wear as opposed to having a nose job done or a tattoo removed.

Making an inventory of attributes

Answer some or all of these questions. Write down your answers quickly. You might want to date the piece of paper for future reference – it can be good to look back later on and realise how quickly the differences you made started to stack up and settle in.

1. What qualities do others attribute to you?

- What qualities have been attributed to you by others? (Think bosses. Think parents and family members. Think teachers. Think colleagues. Think friends.)
- What do these attributed qualities seem to rule in for you, and what do they rule out?
- How much do you feel your behaviour, and your sense of who you are, has been shaped by them? What effect might they be having on who you could be, or would like to be?

2. What attributes do you assume for yourself?

Earlier, I mentioned 'internal dialogue', the way you talk to yourself. Often, this follows on from the attributed qualities others have given you, and it can become taken for granted – effectively 'unheard' – in much the same way.

- It may not be quite so easy to jot down how you think about yourself, but have a go. You're looking for 'I'm the kind of person who . . .' statements or variations like, 'I can/can't do that because I'm an X kind of person' – in other words, trying to winkle out the way you describe yourself to yourself (and thereby discover what attributes you are reinforcing).
- Over the next few days, try to keep an ear open for similar kinds of statements you make out loud to others, particularly when explaining the way you behave or your approach to things. Jot these down too.

Making changes

Which of these attributes would you like to change? As with managing other mammoth issues, look for small differences you can make through changing your behaviour or your way of thinking.

Now pick the tool for the job

There are some powerful tools at your disposal – and remember, you are looking for the greatest results with least effort.

1. Pattern-interrupt

As I've explained before (see p. 56) this technique is a powerful one and has many applications, which is why it should often spring to your mind. As far as reshaping self-image is concerned, analyse any patterns that keep you short of a wanted commodity or result in too much of an undesired one. Include your own habits of thinking and internal dialogue as well as 'scripts' (repeating actions and dialogue) that involve others.

Then identify key moments, such as choice-points, where breaking your usual pattern could derail the familiar process and open up the way for different results. See what happens ... Did this make the difference you hoped for? If so, what was your winning 'recipe'? If not, what other strategies could you experiment with?

2. Modelling

I talked about modelling earlier in the book (see pp. 146–7). Study someone who already possesses the commodity you want. Become a naturalist – observe yourself and others in detail to identify the behaviour or skills you could usefully model. You want to do more than just copy them, of course: you want to remain you, but a 'you' who benefits from the qualities your model possesses. To achieve this, you'll need to incorporate key features of your model's behaviour and thinking into your own way of doing things. You'll need, though, to remember that modelling only works when it enhances the real, authentic you. Think of it as a strategy that can help you express your deeper self. Otherwise, it's just mimicking, and convinces nobody – not even you!

A client of mine wanted to be taken more seriously at work. He thought carefully about the colleagues he knew to be most influential – in particular, how they behaved in meetings. He had good ideas and relevant information, but he didn't get listened to, whereas they did. So what did they do differently that got them listened to? How did they present themselves? How did they move? What sort of voice tone and tempo of speech did they use?

Analysing his models in this way gave my client a behavioural profile he could adapt for his own use. And – surprise surprise! – modelling influential people in his own way soon got people listening to him in a way they never had before. Careful changes at a behavioural level brought about significant differences in how he was perceived and felt about himself – the level of identity.

Once you too start thinking like this, you may be surprised just how much information you already have.

In order to model effectively, you're going to have to compare and contrast. You know your model has more of the commodity you want than you currently do. Compare the way they behave with the way you do in key situations. Just how do you and they compare? My client pinpointed some significant differences in speech speed and tone, as well as in movement and posture, which he was able to use to modify how he acted in the situations that mattered. Don't forget things like personal style.

> **Don't delete as you observe – any detail might be the key you need.**

If you have the kind of connection with someone that allows you to ask them personal questions, try to find out what they are thinking, as well as what they actually do, and compare the way you and they think about such situations before, during and after the event. This can give you really valuable information that will help you emulate their effectiveness. It could be what they are saying to themselves, the images they are seeing in their heads, or the feelings they are tapping into. Perhaps they are using these to evoke past successes, to encourage themselves or to visualise the outcomes they want for the future. You could do the same.

3. Stacking up useful memories, experiences and messages

Past experiences can have a huge impact, positive or negative, on your self-image and the way you interact with others. I have often been amazed how many of my clients lacked self-confidence, even though they held down skilled, responsible and important jobs. Often, it was small things from the past that were dogging their progress. If you want to build a commodity like confidence or authority, take a few moments to think back to try to discover how you came to have less of it than you'd like.

Parents and teachers – even well-meaning ones – can often be the culprits here. Deep down, you may remember looking silly, or being told off in public, when you were young, and unconsciously avoid situations where that might happen again nowadays. Or you may have internalised a belief held by someone else and acted according to it. 'People like us don't expect that' or, 'Don't tell others how good you are – that's boasting and nice people don't boast.' Are beliefs like these really serving *you, now?* Or are they keeping you stuck in attribute thinking?

Using anchors to help create a stock of the commodity you want

You can start building up your stock of a desired commodity such as feeling confident or capable by collecting up all sorts of small experiences and examples that make you feel that way. In NLP, this connection between small external things (objects, sounds, memories, words, for example) and important internal feelings is called 'anchoring'.

One of my clients ran a successful small company, but still lacked confidence in her own ability. I asked her to write down on separate Post-it notes every compliment that she could remember having received, and asked her to stick them randomly around the house where she couldn't help but keep seeing them. Each time she noticed one, she was to say it to herself, and notice how it made her feel. The Post-it notes were a visual anchor for the compliments, which were themselves written or spoken anchors that she had been ignoring. Repeated exposure to these compliments in their anchored format helped her begin to believe there must be some truth in them, so that she began growing her stock of self-confidence.

Another client who was prone to anxiety told me that he would feel so much better if only his wife were with him in his difficult and sometimes dangerous work – she really made him feel supported. Even though she couldn't be with him in person, a handkerchief with her perfume on it could be in his pocket to remind him of her love and support. And for him, that tangible anchor for a whole range of important and supportive emotions made all the difference.

The simpler and sweeter anchoring experiences are the better. Think of a place, sound or idea that makes you feel calm and good in yourself. Go over and over it in your mind, until you find something about it that really seems to sum it up. Perhaps it's a phrase of words or music, or a tiny detail of something you saw or felt. Relish it. Ingrain it. Play it over and over. Practise thinking of that single small thing and letting it bring back all the rest – this is what can help you create and strengthen a deliberately created anchor. It could be the sound of a loved voice saying your name. Or the smile on your dog's face when you get home. Or the glow of personal triumph you felt when you completed a difficult project.

Next time you are about to go into a situation you expect to find stressful or challenging, prepare for it by calling up your positive anchor and its good feelings. The more you use it, the stronger and more effective it will become.

Weakening unhelpful anchors

Some anchors can bring up negative feelings. You can safely and effectively work on your own to erode anchors that connect with mildly unpleasant or debilitating commodities, though more powerful or disabling feelings may be best approached with the support of a professional counsellor or therapist.

TRY THIS:

- In writing, tell the story of how your unwanted commodity originally came to be linked to its anchor.
- Write it in the third person (he/she not I/we). This helps distance the nowadays-you from the there-and-then victim of the experience that you used to be.
- Put your story firmly in the past tense, rather than the present, using phrases such as 'she said', 'he used to', 'she once', 'people tended to'. This is a clear message in itself: it's the implied equivalent of *once upon a time ...*
- Make your storyline silly, funny, filmic or cartoonish if you can – all these approaches tend to destabilise the effect of the start-up event.
- With a different colour of pen or type, go through your original story adding in things that change the impact or even the events. For example, give helpful comments to the reader such as, 'Of course, everyone now knows that ...' or add in what you would like to

▶

have said or done, if only you had had the wit and courage at the time. For example, '"Mean bastard," I said under my breath' or, 'I turned away as though I hadn't heard' or, 'I reached for my mobile and immediately dialled his manager to register my complaint.'

You know perfectly well that none of these things is 'true' in the sense of having actually happened – but then how true is it that you are as silly nowadays as the eight-year-old whose mum told him off, or whose teacher wrote such a scathing report, or whose boss tore his proposal to shreds in front of the rest of the team? You have been behaving and feeling as if these things were true. Why not swap out a damaging, self-limiting fiction for a useful, enabling one?

When you feel inadequate or when someone in authority makes you feel stressed or afraid, imagining them in a situation where they look ridiculous can often help: it's as though you've overlaid them with a different image. Since it's difficult to hold two contradictory ideas about someone at the same time, the process helps destabilise the image that puts you off. In John le Carré's *Tinker Tailor Soldier Spy*, his hero Smiley's wife Ann describes deflating someone's importance by imagining them as a toad.

Changing self-image can feel like a real beast of a mammoth. But the good news is that each of these strategies can help you achieve the simple underlying issue: turning attributes into commodities. Commodities can grow. You can reshape yourself. If you want to change again in the future, you can: you are not a fixed but a growing, evolving creature. And that's pretty exciting.

So far, we've explored how you can recognise both your mammoth and your in-built style of approaching it and looked at ways of tackling those beasts you'd like to get under control.

Now it's time to discover how the skills you've been developing can be applied with even greater subtlety and finesse by making the best use of your best times. In particular, I'll show you how to combine your chunking skills with fine timing to deal with issues affecting work, study, health and wellbeing. And that's the subject I'll move on to in Section Four.

SECTION FOUR

Finishing Touches

12

Optimum Times, Optimum Timing

During the course of the book so far, I've provided you with a tool-kit for understanding, approaching and getting to grips with life's most common mammoths. What more do you need? This section of the book gives you some very important and powerful information that takes you beyond basic mammoth-management to managing mammoths with subtlety and refinement, making it easier to achieve even more with even less effort.

As a start, let's return to you, the mammoth-manager.

When are you at your best?

I explained in Chapter 3 how important it is to know what your best distance is – that is, whether you are a sprinter or a middle- or long-distancer. But there's a further refinement you can add to your self-knowledge. Irrespective of your natural style of attack, there will also be certain times of day when you function at your best. Knowing when these are and working with, rather than against, them can give you an extra edge when dealing with any mammoth.

Check yourself out

Perhaps you've already worked out whether you are a 'lark' or an 'owl' – in other words, whether you're at your most alert in the morning or in the evening.

- Do you feel bright and energetic as soon as your eyes open? You're probably a Lark (L).
- Do you feel at your best in the evening and late at night? You could be an Owl (O).
- Do you tend to drop off to sleep after your evening meal? (L)
- If you're immersed in a book, watching a video or concentrating on something, could you keep going into the early hours without feeling tired or drowsy? (O)

Whether you are a lark or an owl, it makes sense to factor rhythms like these into how you plan your days. In particular, when important projects are involved – whether at home or at work – bear in mind that you're likely to think more crisply, concentrate better and generally achieve more when you work at something during your natural 'best' times of high energy and sharp focus.

Though they're different in many ways, Larks and Owls both tend to experience a 'dip' in energy and alertness after lunch. It's a reminder that despite all our centuries of civilisation, we are still animals: after they've eaten, all animals tend to divert their energies into digesting their food. If you

were a boa constrictor, you might doze for days! Your dog
or cat will sleep for several hours unless it's disturbed. It's
natural for human beings to do the same – though in recent
years it's become part of office culture in some highly driven
kinds of employment to work through lunch or munch it at
your desk.

When I first started to coach investment bankers, I was
horrified to find that none of them expected to take a
lunch break. I told them I wasn't going to work through
my lunchtime and arranged my appointments to give
myself a mid-day break. I knew I needed a time of gearing-
down, and I hoped they'd learn from my example. I'm
pretty sure they put it down as another of my eccentric-
ities: the work culture had already got them. It wasn't
just a characteristic of banking: I have to say that I
have found much the same obtaining in some parts of
the NHS!

Ignoring your body's natural rhythms means you are
ignoring your own deeply in-built self-knowledge. Do this
for long enough and your mind and body will fight back.

I remember one day having a series of coaching appointments in the afternoon, and one by one, all my bright
young clients came in – and then started dropping off to
sleep. They apologised for their tiredness, offering quite
understandable reasons: the kids woke me up; the wife
had a cold; I had a late meeting and couldn't switch off ...
I believed every one of them – but I also knew that over
the weeks and the months and even, in some cases, the

years, they had been overriding the messages from within that said: *stop and rest right now!*

Research is showing us increasingly that driven lifestyles, like those of these young people, can cause damage that's not just immediate, but cumulative. Stress itself becomes a habit, affecting the mind and the emotions, as well as the body. A tired mind doesn't concentrate so well as a fresh one, so tasks take longer and consume even more energy. A tired mind and body aren't so resilient when something challenging comes up or when something goes wrong. Tempers fray. Sharp words are spoken. I have known competent professionals freeze, cry or even hit out when something in itself quite innocuous tipped the balance and became in a second their own particular 'final straw'.

TRY THIS:

Here are some quick exercises to release and refresh you. Try at least one today. You can do them at your workplace, as well as at home, provided you find somewhere a bit private or somewhere there are so many people you won't be noticed. Crowded places like cafeteria queues or public spaces between buildings can be quite good places for you to be temporarily invisible!

These exercises will only take a short time, yet the results are disproportionately beneficial. Remember the myth that big achievements require big effort and take lots of time? Myth. Repeat – myth!

▶

If you can, take a minimum of fifteen minutes off (preferably more) at least twice during the day to refresh and re-energise yourself by doing one or more of the following.

- You could get up and walk about. If possible, go outside for a few minutes. Look at something natural – the clouds, the pigeons strutting about (unless urban pigeons make you wild, that is!), other people doing their thing. Be a camera. Be curious about the world around you, in a laid-back kind of way.

- Raise your shoulders as high as they will go, hold them there for a few moments, then let them slide gently down again, flattening out your shoulder blades as they go. Without even trying, you are likely to let out a deep sigh as this happens. If you're worried about being observed, clench your hands into fists and your feet into claws: hold the clench and your breath for a few moments, then let everything open, let go and spread out again.

- Put a hand on your belly just below your bottom ribs, and take in a big enough breath to feel your newly inflated lungs pushing your hand outwards. Hold for a few seconds, then let your breath out slowly, feeling your hand moving back in again. Repeat several times.

Introducing your ultradian rhythms

It's natural for all of us to experience a regular daily pattern of alternations between the times of higher and lower energy. These daily swings can arrive gently, almost unobtrusively, or be quite marked, even dramatic. But this isn't all. Operating within these once-a-day patterns of action and rest, known as *circadian rhythms,* there are shorter ones whose effects are just as universal and important. These patterns are known as *ultradian rhythms* and were first identified by R. Klein and R. Armitage in their 1979 research paper published in *Science* magazine – 'Rhythms in human performance: one-and-a-half-hour oscillations in cognitive style'.

Ultradian rhythms have a shorter rise-and-fall pattern than the daily circadian ones. Every ninety minutes or so, they orchestrate a complete mind–body cycle of activity and rest, which includes changing activities even at the level of molecules and hormones. This pattern has been called the Basic Rest Activity Cycle (BRAC), and even when we are asleep, its rhythms govern the depth of our sleeping and the frequency of our dreams. This is one reason why depriving someone of sleep can derail them not only physically, but emotionally and mentally: we need to be able to sleep deeply because it's in deep sleep that the body rests and repairs itself, and we also have an emotional and psychological need to dream because dreaming helps us to sort out and shape our experiences at an unconscious level.

What tells us where we are within an ultradian cycle? It's fairly easy for us to spot when we're in the peak part of our cycle: we feel bright, energised and focused. During this time, we often rely on our left-brain logic and rational, step-by-step methods to approach tasks and achieve our goals.

Less easy to spot and celebrate are the corresponding dips that make up the other half of the cycle. In his innovative work with hypnosis, Milton Erickson found that most healing progress could be made when clients spontaneously dropped into a 'naturalistic trance' of outward stillness and inward reflection. The psychobiology of the trance state seems to help activate right-brain (associative, creative, non-linear) ways of thinking, which may be an important reason why trance can aid creative ways of understanding and come up with solutions that the rational, left-brain, conscious thinking can't. In his book, *The 20-Minute Break*, Erickson's editor and colleague Ernest Rossi says:

> We can observe this same 90–120 minute basic rest–activity cycle operating in us twenty-four hours a day. It is responsible for the patterns of arousal, peak performance, stress, and recovery that we experience every few hours. Just as we average a 20-minute dream period every 90 to 120 minutes during sleep, we have similar periods while awake when we are more prone to fantasy, daydreams, inner focus, and rejuvenation.

The very rhythm of our days is the simplest way to spot how these cycles are operating – if we will attend to it.

We are all familiar with the roughly two-hourly 'dips' afforded by breakfast, mid-morning break time, lunch, teatime, evening mealtime and perhaps also bedtime snack-time. These dips are woven into the fabric of organisational as well as personal life, and when they are observed, can help us function in harmony with our psychobiological need for rest and recharging. However, both at home and – especially – in the workplace we tend to value the peaks more highly.

We all experience ultradian cycles, though sometimes because of pressure, convenience or sheer sense of drive we may try to ignore or override them. Yet people often don't realise how important the dips are: many may think of them as a 'falling-off' from their 'real' or 'best' level of alertness and energy, rather than recognising them as an essential means of recharging. We need to accept that these fluctuations are essential to our proper functioning, and to realise not only how powerful it can be to work in harmony with them, but also how counter-productive – sometimes even damaging – it can be to work against them.

TRY THIS:

- As you go through the day, jot down the times when you take a break (loo stops, getting yourself a coffee or tea, having lunch, etc.).
- Try to monitor your state of alertness. Jot down any times when you felt fresh and focused, and others when you felt slow, spacey or sleepy. Any idea how long each of these patches lasted?
- Did you go along with your natural state or try to override it? What were the results of working in or out of harmony with your state?

Monitoring your own natural rhythms over a few days will quickly help you establish your baseline patterns, so that you can more easily recognise when you're working with or against them. When, for example, circumstances have forced you to override your need for dip times. This self-awareness will also give you the extra argument you may need to convince yourself (or others) that it's now time to restore your self-harmony and freshness again.

Working longer isn't necessarily working better

Think again about that 90- to 120-minute ultradian cycle. Since the dip lasts only about twenty minutes, there will be quite a lot of time in any cycle which is spent either building up from it towards the next peak or powering down from a previous peak towards the next dip. We know from other research that full concentration (one of the characteristics of a peak) only lasts for about forty-five minutes at a time: after that it tails off as the powering-down phase begins and the next dip gets closer. People often refer to 'peak performance', but often this phrase is used to mean being on 'top form', without the corresponding recognition that sooner or later every peak is followed by a dip. Nobody can be at peak performance for hours at a time. Once you're off the peak, your concentration dissipates – and, almost inevitably, the quality of your performance falls off with it. Perhaps we should instead talk about 'best performance', which involves utilising both the peaks and the dips to their full effect.

My bright, ambitious young city clients (and their employers, sadly) made the mistake of thinking that long hours equalled hard work. Twelve-hour days were the norm – and the cause of many undesired results such as sleepiness, anxiety, irritability and probably also of the emotional volatility and knee-jerk reactivity that's so characteristic of the financial markets.

Respecting ultradian cycles in everyday life

What can you do about this? Real life doesn't allow us to chop our working days up into convenient little slices, and it would be tedious and difficult to try. But we can each be mindful of these variations and try to work along with them, rather than against them.

When I was a student revising for my Finals, I did try to study for a straight eight hours each day, and I'm sure this contributed to the exhaustion and stress I experienced. When I was a postgraduate, I had more friends and less sense of urgency to do well, so my working time was much more broken up. Social life was much more important and work had to fit into it and around it. As a result, I was less stressed and – surprise surprise! – performed much better.

If you take the twenty-minute dip and the forty-five-minute concentration peak as affording the ideal climate for different and necessary kinds of mental and physical activity, you can begin to see that each ultradian cycle contains serious opportunities for contrasting ways of focusing. In short, every 90 to 120 minutes you get a peak-performance high, affording you good concentration, with tails at either end for powering up and slowing down, and then a twenty-minute soft-focus dip, which could repair and refresh you because it carries the potential for differently organised inner work.

It's easier for us to recognise and celebrate the 'peaks'. Peak alertness helps you manage task-type mammoths and delivers best value as far as goal-driven tasks and challenges are concerned. Yet dip-time states allow you essential rest, restoration and inner reflection, as Milton Erickson's collaborator Ernest Rossi reminded us when he said:

> The ultradian relaxation response may be the most practical, effective, psychobiological means we have at present for accessing and potentiating healing and rejuvenation of mind–body processes.

Why does a peak last roughly twice as long as a dip? I doubt if anyone knows. But my intuitive theory is that it's something to do with the fact that conscious activity processes material logically and sequentially, while unconscious activity processes it more rapidly through shorter associative pathways.

In terms of getting the best out of yourself, all you need to remember is that peaks are best for concentration and focus and their height lasts about forty-five minutes; dips are best for reflection, healing and creativity and last about twenty minutes.

Once you've worked out where you fit on the broad spectrum of Owl versus Lark, take a closer look at your personal 'map' of the day's energy. Where you can, try to schedule high-energy, high-focus tasks for your peak times. If you need to collaborate with colleagues, try to find out where their peaks occur too. You might train yourself to observe the states other people are in through watching the physical signs of high or low energy, intent or soft focusing, which they'll give out quite unconsciously. In terms of building rapport and effective collaboration, dovetail with others where you can.

Over to You

Here are my step-by-step instructions for beginning the process of inner rest and reflection. I think of it as an 'Over to You' (that's you talking to your inner self) appeal to resourceful hidden depths. If you have twenty minutes free, you can try it out today, and hopefully begin a whole new, life-enhancing habit by doing so.

1. Take the opportunity of a dip to do some personal work.
When you're tired, irritable, or simply feel the need to take a break, recognise it as a dip and therefore an opportunity to establish personal harmony and do some internal rebalancing and healing.

Find yourself a private and comfortable space where you can sit or lie down and tune into yourself. With practice, you'll soon be able to do it anywhere that you can switch off: travelling on trains, buses and the tube, waiting in checkout queues ...

Have it in your mind that you'll give yourself about

twenty minutes – most people have a really accurate 'internal timer'. If you're worried you'll fall asleep for ages, first set the alarm on your watch or phone for half-an-hour's time. That way, you've a failsafe – but by adding some extra time you are also giving yourself the chance to discover how reliable that internal timer can be.

2. Access and utilise your inner resources. Tune in to your body. Which part of you is feeling most comfortable? Explore that feeling of comfort and notice how it spreads and deepens as you concentrate on it.

3. Imagine a private place you can retreat to. You can use a real place – current or from your past – or a totally imagined one. What would make you feel safe and comfortable there? Might you want to feel pampered, or stimulated? Is it indoors or outdoors? Does it have weather, scenery or furniture? How do you get there, and return again? People I've worked with over the years have used towers, beaches, gardens and favourite childhood hidey-holes. They have been transported by lifts, planes, rockets and flights of stairs.

4. Become curious about how your unconscious might use this time. Allow yourself to wonder idly how you will tap into your reservoir of experience and knowledge and your in-built ability to rebalance, refresh and renew, so as to help you deal with current issues and problems more effectively than you ever expected. You may begin to feel sleepy. You might even fall asleep.

5. Come back to the 'real' world. After about twenty minutes, you'll notice that you're 'awake' and aware of yourself, but somehow you were not a moment ago. If you have been asleep, don't assume that the self-work and self-healing weren't happening. They don't need you conscious for that! You are likely to be curious about what the results of your time-out will be. Sometimes ideas and insights snap into view immediately, but more often they just 'arrive' in your conscious awareness over the next few hours and days.

Now you might want to stand up and stretch, or just stare into space for a moment or two as you reorientate to the everyday world.

6. Make this personal work a habitual part of your life. Knowing how helpful good habits can be, make an agreement with yourself to take another time-out in the next few days – and then another. The effects will be cumulative!

Other opportunities for encouraging dip work

As we've seen, ultradian dips occur naturally roughly every 90 to 120 minutes. But certain activities can also encourage a similar mind–body state. You can make use of these too. They include:

- repetitive physical activities that occupy you while allowing your mind to free-float such as running, walking, ironing or knitting and
- routine tasks that you're very familiar with, such as showering, gardening, driving, washing-up. Though these contain a greater variety of physical activity and a

certain amount of decision-making, they all give you a degree of mental distance and quite long periods of open focus.

Working in harmony with your ultradian rhythms: a summary

1. Know when you're most alert (Lark or Owl).
2. Make the most of both your optimum concentration span (ninety minutes, of which forty-five are peak focus) and your optimum reflection or dip time (twenty minutes).
3. Know the kind of mammoth you're dealing with, and which approach best suits it.
4. Use conscious, left-brain processing for logical, rational, well-defined tasks and tap into natural dips to encourage right-brain processing, reflection, healing and rebalancing.

Working in harmony with your peaks and troughs clears the way for stress-free performance and effortless personal rebalancing.

Finesse can take time to acquire, but the more you apply it, the more of a habit it becomes and the easier it gets. Expertise is cumulative, as are self-awareness and self-knowledge. But there's still more you can do. The 'twenty-minute miracles' that form the subject of the next, and final, chapter are the result of unconscious, right-brain processing that goes naturally with dip-time space and inward dip-time reflection. That's why something as life-transforming as a miracle can actually happen in twenty minutes.

13

Twenty-minute Miracles

In a sense, this whole book has been about miracles. The first and most important one is each of us. We are truly astonishing. The second miracle is that, alone among living creatures, we have the ability to consider ourselves from the outside, as well as from the inside – in other words, to be self-aware and to self-reflect. And the third miracle, which derives from the first two, is that we are able to manage ourselves – in other words, to self-shape and self-evolve.

The root meaning of the word 'miracle' is 'something to be wondered at'. As I explained in the previous chapter, the speed and elegance with which we are all capable of making significant changes in our feeling, thinking and behaviour can seem miraculous – but the truly miraculous thing is that *this ability is in-built*.

Real miracles can happen not in minutes but in seconds: that's all it takes to change your mind, see something from a new angle or do something different. These miracles can happen anywhere as a result of using your dip times, not just for rest and rebalancing, but to access a different kind of brain processing from your usual conscious analysis and planning. Miracles can happen on the bus, on the way home from school, in the shower, in the checkout queue, staring at the ceiling from the dentist's chair or the hairdresser's wash-basin. In the blink of an eye or the taking of a breath.

You don't even need twenty minutes – but if you give yourself the luxury of that amount of time, you can even be relaxed while you're about it. The miracle-inducing processes explained in this chapter work because:

- Your mind can work incredibly fast.
- You're committed to managing that mammoth from now on.
- You know that mammoth-managing doesn't take oodles of time, incredible strength or mind-blowing effort. It takes equipment you already have and now know you can rely on – the ability to manage *yourself* differently before you try to make a start on your mammoth itself.

Don't assume that just because something is important it needs your peak attention. Peaks are often associated with conscious, left-brain, logical thinking and organisa-tion; but if you want to find new ways through old problems, generate new ideas or get into right-brain, intu-itive, lateral thinking, you're best to harness your dips and let your conscious mind wander and your thoughts float idly from one thing to another (a process sometimes called 'wool-gathering'). If you allow yourself to 'go with the flow', you will, of course, be in 'dip' mode; but it's useful to know that such natural 'altered states' of awareness not only allow you to rest, but also give you a potential hotline to your unconscious, non-rational, non-sequential mental processing. This is the part of your mind that 'just knows', that takes unscheduled leaps and bounds and just presents you with ideas 'out of nowhere'. Or should I be saying 'out of know-where'? Left-brain ideas usually arrive as the result of a deliberate process of 'thinking through' (and that everyday, taken-for-granted phrase just shows that we all recognise that this is how it goes). Right-brain ideas, on the other hand, rocket up from the deeps and usually arrive with no obvious connection to what you're doing or think-ing at the time. But when they arrive, they usually 'feel right', however disconnected.

Right-brain processing happens all the time; but you can deliberately 'invite it in' during these natural dip times just by flagging up the 'headline' of an issue in your mind – in much the same way as you might type it on a blank screen or scribble it at the top of a new sheet of paper. 'What can I do about …?' 'What's the next step with …?' 'What on earth is going on when …?' Such a headline thought, registered deliberately at a time of natural dip, is often all you need to set off a whole train of innovative, right-brain processing, which is just what you want when your mammoth has your conscious, left-brain thinking stuck, puzzled or running out of ideas. Continuing to bash away at the same old approaches you've tried (and failed with) before is out: time for your own different way of thinking to come in. You will know at once if your new approach has delivered the goods. As the iconic American thriller writer Raymond Chandler put it in *The Little Sister*:

And the little bell rang, the one that rings far back at the end of the corridor, and is not so loud, but you'd better hear it. No matter what other noises there are you'd better hear it.

Dip-time miracles

So how can you access that right-brain part of yourself, and what miracles can you perform with those twenty-minute slots of dip that offer themselves to you every day without fail?

First of all, you'll need to give yourself a physical and mental space where you can disconnect from other concerns and be passively attentive to yourself. The 'messages' you receive from that different part of your brain may come in the form of words (though often single words and phrases, rather than full sentences), pictures or physical sensations (lightness, heaviness, blankness, buzz...). The only job your conscious, left-brain processing needs to perform is the 'highlighting' of the issue you want your right brain to work on. You don't need to 'think through' your issue, just flag it up and wait.

Brainstormers

One good way to generate new ways of managing your mammoth is to let yourself brainstorm. Focus on your heading, then rapidly list *every* possibility that comes into your mind – do not censor or attempt to evaluate on grounds of practicality or good sense. Among your quick-fire, idiotic, amusing, impossible ideas, there may just be one that will surprise you and actually work. It can be useful to set a timer – the pressure of that artificial deadline stops you engaging your rational, critical left brain.

On a recent course on 'getting your novel published' the tutors asked people to brainstorm ten new titles for their novel in five minutes. (Setting an apparently 'impossible' time frame for such a task helped bypass people's left-brain thinking and access their right-brain creativity.) Then the students read these new titles out aloud in small groups (without saying what the novel was about) in order to test how intriguing others found them. As a result, many of the writers abandoned the working title they had arrived with and took up one of those they had brainstormed instead.

Model someone different

As I explained earlier in the book (see pp. 180–2), modelling someone else can be a powerful way to understand and acquire a new skill. Think of someone you know who is very different from you. You don't necessarily have to choose someone you think would be better at dealing with your mammoth – just use your imagination to get into a different skin for a few moments to discover how your mammoth looks from another perspective and how else it might be approached.

Tales of the gods and heroes

When I was a child, I had a book with this title. It reminds us that when modelling desired behaviour or different approaches, we don't have to limit ourselves to people we actually know. Imagine your task or ambition as a challenge faced by one of your personal heroes. You might choose someone from history or legend who inspires you, or someone alive today. Think yourself into their skin. Briefly write the legend of how they faced your challenge and came through victorious. Be bold, use overblown language, ham it up. How do you feel about your challenge now – and what tips did you gain from your hero?

Pan for the nugget

This is a three-step exercise, but it still only takes twenty minutes, and like the novel-title exercise referred to on p. 211, it uses the urgency of working to tight times to help you bypass conscious analytical thinking and stimulate your right-brain self-knowledge instead. Set a timer (watch, phone or kitchen varieties would all do for this) for ten minutes.

1. Write down everything you can think of about your mammoth as fast as you can and without trying to make sense, deliberating or editing. Do not stop writing till the timer goes.
2. Next, without reading through what you've written, set the timer again, this time for seven minutes. Make a bulleted list of the key ways in which your mammoth bugs you.

3. Next, and again without rereading, set the timer for three minutes. Write down one point only – what's the central core of your mammoth problem?

   Start working from there!

Name your aim

Many people don't realise that we all have an in-built, internal timer and that we can 'set it' deliberately. You can set your internal timer for twenty minutes before you start your internal journey. You might do this by saying the words 'twenty minutes' to yourself, or imagine two clock faces side by side, with a twenty-minute difference between them. Or, of course, you can invent your own method. Have a question or an aim in mind as you begin – e.g. 'I really need to rest deeply for a while' or 'I'd like to use this time to find a new way of achieving/approaching/looking at X.'

Rotation, rotation

Imagine your mammoth as if it were an object in front of you (you could even just think of an actual hairy mammoth as its temporary representative). If it's really scary, create a nice strong corral around it, so there's a barrier between you and it, keeping you safe. Now take a walk around it, so that you see it from every angle. Look at it close up and from far away. You are likely to notice some aspects or details you haven't spotted before. How might these help you in managing it differently or better?

Powerful questions you can ask yourself

I've already introduced you to what psychotherapists call 'the miracle question' (see p. 157). There are a number of other powerful questions coaches use to help people take a different look at something or tap into unconscious knowledge they have without yet knowing they have it.

The questions are levers in themselves, so you can ask them of yourself and surprise yourself with the extent of their leverage and your inner understanding. You could use your dip time for these or you could just raise a question with yourself at any time and any place, and trust that the answer will come to you later on. Take one question at a time: your answers may come from either full left-brain logic and rigour or rich, reflective right-brain mulling. You might even explore the same question at different times in different ways to build a more complex picture.

Think carefully about each and every word as you ask the question of yourself – one reason they can be so effective is that every word counts in its own right. Here are some of the best:

In relation to my mammoth

- *What is the biggest challenge I face?*
- *What is the biggest risk I might take?*
- *What would my greatest satisfaction be?*
- *What or who can I rely on?*

This first group of questions gets you to refine the nature and dimension of the mammoth. The following questions enable you to explore the challenges you are dealing with in more depth.

- *So what's really going on here?*
  This moves you away from the 'story' to the underlying issue or principle.

- *Whose problem actually is it?*
  Sometimes someone else has 'given' you their problem. It might even have been unintentionally given to you years ago by parents, teachers or friends. Perhaps it's time to hand it back or just put it down.

- *What do I really want?*
  This question is one to ask when you feel you're flapping around or stuck in the present because it helps focus you on the longer term.

- *What really matters here?*
  Boil it down. Cut to the chase. Cut out the crap.

- *Who really matters here?*
  It could be you – your survival is at stake. It could be someone else. Perhaps it's the planet. Your call.

- *Who says so?*
  The poet Coleridge had a great phrase to describe the kind of authority in the background that badgers all of us from time to time. He called it 'ancient voices prophesying war'. Often, the things we think or believe originate from our own thinking and experience aren't ours at all. This question gets you testing out whether you really think or believe or want whatever it is. Have

you taken someone else's stuff on board? Once you know, you are in a better position to decide whether or not you want to take personal ownership of it now. Either way, it could substantially affect how you manage your mammoth in the future.

- *Where does this fit?*
  If you're thinking of something detailed, this question invites you to chunk up and see how it slots into the bigger picture. If you're stuck on the bigger picture, this asks you to chunk down to details.

- *And then ...?*
  What's the next bit of the action likely to be?

- *And in five years' time ...?*
  What are the longer-term effects and implications? You may not get your forecast right in every detail – that's the lot of many a forecaster, since we can't know everything in advance – but asking the question reminds you that there *will* be consequences that far ahead. Imagine several scenarios, and try to work round or develop strategies now for unwanted possibilities then.

- *On my deathbed I'll be really pleased that ...*

- *On my deathbed I'd really regret it if I hadn't ...*
  These two focus your attention on the opportunities you have right now to manage your mammoth, shape your future and heal your past. Choice only happens in the present, but by framing it in the light of our last moments we sharpen our sense of present-moment opportunity.

The single most decisive part of managing your mammoth is *choosing to manage it*. When you do that and how you do it is up to you. I hope you believe now, even if you didn't before you read this book, that you do have what it takes to tame that mammoth of yours.

As you experiment, reflect and refine your managerial skills, you'll discover more about yourself and your own resourcefulness. Mammoths are an inevitable part of human life. This book is not about making them go away, but about being more able to deal with them. In a strange way, taking on the challenge of your mammoth may do more than just get it under control: it may change the way you see and feel about yourself for ever.

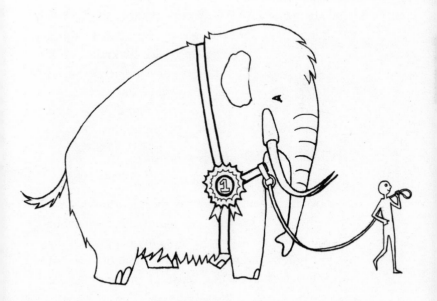

Acknowledgments

This book owes a lot to the discipline of NLP in two senses. It makes use of the NLP concept of 'chunking up and down' as a straightforward tool for making life's mammoth tasks, problems and ambitions manageable. And in the essential NLP manner, it draws upon the personal 'recipes' of individuals to illustrate how this can be done.

People are at the core of NLP: among its central presuppositions are two that particularly apply here. First, people do the best they can; and, second, there is a discoverable, personal structure to both success and failure. When we uncover these underlying structures in our own way of going about things, we can begin to do more of what works and less of what doesn't. We can also 'borrow' (in the NLP word, 'model') the patterns that work well for others and begin to make them our own.

In a very real sense, this book is built with the help of NLP, but it also draws on long experience working with altered states of consciousness, both naturally occurring and formally created using hypnosis. Its diverse building

Acknowledgments

materials have been brought together from all the different venues of my life, and it's furnished throughout by the struggles and successes of my clients. During a career of over forty years, working with a huge range of different people in contexts ranging from universities to therapy rooms and the offices of public-sector organisations and multi-national businesses, I have been fortunate enough to meet and learn from wonderful, imaginative, dogged, persistent, creative, thoughtful, caring and successful people. Many of them would have been amazed to hear themselves so described. Their learning has enriched and informed mine, and shines through every page of this book. Some of their stories are told here, disguised and adapted to preserve their confidentiality and protect their vulnerability. We are all vulnerable in the face of our mammoths.

More specifically, I owe more than I can say to the support and practical help of some very special people. My husband, Leo, and my friend Su Reid, both of whom read every chapter as it was written and helped me get it clearer and more reader-friendly. My daughter Charlotte, my friends Jan Russell, Jane Lemmon, Amanda Prout and Liz Marks, who encouraged me throughout. Gill Bailey at Piatkus, who shared my excitement at the original idea of Bite-sizing, and Claudia Dyer who actually commissioned and edited the manuscript with her usual flair for both small- and large-chunk comments. Thanks also to Anne Newman for her invaluable help in finalising the text.

Finally, a particular thank you to Kathryn Miller, whose drawings made the mammoth itself come to life – a former threat made tame in our hands.

Further Explorations

Explore Milton Erickson

Jay Haley, *Uncommon Therapy: the psychiatric techniques of Milton H. Erickson*, W. W. Norton & Co., 1973

Sidney Rosen (ed.), *My Voice Will Go with You: the teaching tales of Milton H. Erickson*, W. W. Norton & Co., 1982

Explore NLP

Richard Bandler, *Using Your Brain for a Change*, Real People Press, 1985

Robert Dilts, *Changing Belief Systems with NLP*, Meta Publications, 1990

Robert B. Dilts, Todd Epstein & Robert W. Dilts, *Tools for Dreamers: strategies for creativity and the structure of innovation*, Meta Publications, 1991

Wendy Jago, *The NLP Brain Builder*, Piatkus, 2010

Ian McDermott & Wendy Jago, *The NLP Coach*, Piatkus, 2001

Explore left-brain and right-brain thinking

Guy Claxton, *Hare Brain, Tortoise Mind: why intelligence increases when you think less*, Fourth Estate, 1997

Further Explorations

Malcolm Gladwell, *Blink: the power of thinking without thinking*, Penguin Books, 2005

Ernest Lawrence Rossi, *The 20-Minute Break*, Jeremy Tarcher, 1991

Ian McDermott & Wendy Jago, *Your Inner Coach*, Piatkus, 2003

Explore personal change

Connirae & Steve Andreas, *Heart of the Mind: engaging your inner power to change with neuro-linguistic programming*, Real People Press, 1989

Leslie Cameron-Bandler, David Gordon & Michael Lebeau, *Know How: guided programs for inventing your own best future*, Real People Press, 1985

Carol S. Dweck, *Mindset: how you can fulfil your potential*, Ballantine Books, 2006

Robert Maurer, *One Small Step Can Change Your Life: the Kaizen way*, Workman Publishing, 2004

Lissanne Oliver, *Sorted: the ultimate guide to organising your life – once and for all*, Hardie Grant Books, 2007

Barbara Sher, *Wishcraft: how to get what you really want*, Ballantine Books, 1979

Explore organisational change

Chip & Dan Heath, *Switch: how to change things when change is hard*, Random House Business Books, 2010

George Kohlrieser, *Hostage at the Table: how leaders can overcome conflict, influence others, and raise performance*, Jossey Bass, 2006

Tom Rath & Donald O. Clifton, *How Full Is Your Bucket? Positive strategies for work and life*, Gallup Press, 2004

If you are interested in finding out more about coaching or training for individuals or businesses, you can visit my website: www.pivotalcoaching.co.uk or email me on wendy@jagoconsulting.eclipse.co.uk

Index

Index

Index

Index

Index

Also available by Wendy Jago, published by Piatkus:

THE NLP COACH

(with Ian McDermott)

In *The NLP Coach* leading NLP trainers Wendy Jago and Ian McDermott provide an effective programme to help you achieve success at work and at home. This comprehensive, practical and user-friendly guide to self-coaching uses powerful NLP (neuro-linguistic programming) techniques to enable you to:

- Enhance your self-esteem
- Build good relationships and improve your communication skills
- Maximise your brain power, accelerate your learning and improve your memory
- Generate health, wealth and happiness
- Manage yourself and others better and make your work more rewarding
- Reach your full potential and become spiritually alive

978 0 7499 2277 1

Also available by Wendy Jago, published by Piatkus:

YOUR INNER COACH

(with Ian McDermott)

The key to success lies in knowing how to get the most out of yourself. But what does this really mean? In *Your Inner Coach* Wendy Jago and Ian McDermott show you how to master the power of your own mind.

The unconscious mind is the best-ever source of wisdom, information and judgement. Jago and McDermott reveal a process of dynamic inquiry called Inner Coaching that will help you learn how to access and communicate with your unconsciousness – and tap into your own wisdom.

In this inspiring and practical book you will discover how to:

- Build self-knowledge
- Access and trust your gut feelings and intuition
- Find out what you really want in life and harness your inner resources
- Become more creative, confident and spontaneous

978 0 7499 2482 9

Also available by Wendy Jago, published by Piatkus:

THE NLP BRAIN BUILDER

Adaptation is crucial if you want to succeed in today's world. *The NLP Brain Builder* enables you to change habitual patterns of filtering and organising information to become more adaptable. Providing simple yet effective NLP (neuro-linguistic programming) techniques and exercises to improve mental flexibility, it helps you to:

- Become a better negotiator
- Improve decision-making and problem-solving
- Increase your capacity to learn
- Manage your time and priorities

Whatever your starting point, Wendy Jago's *The NLP Brain Builder* will show you how to build mental agility, increasing your chances of surviving and thriving in a world of change, challenge and opportunity.

978 0 7499 4104 8